Honoured as a member of *Travel + Leisure*'s Hall of Fame
and *Condé Nast Traveler*'s Platinum Circle

"The Pointe restaurant at the Wickaninnish Inn was the catalyst [behind
the food scene] in Tofino. Back when it opened in 1996, local, seasonal
eating was very much the exception rather than the rule.... Almost 20
years later, that adherence to local ingredients is no longer a novelty. It's
the default philosophy for almost every dish in Tofino."
CHRIS JOHNS, *The Globe and Mail*

"Tofino's gourmet focus began 15 years ago with the opening of the
smart Pointe restaurant at the Wickaninnish Inn, an elegant Relais &
Châteaux hotel where folk feast on local cod with a romesco crumble
while overlooking the roaring Pacific Ocean."
ROSIE BIRKETT, *Condé Nast Traveler*

"The Pointe has great views. But the food, from chef Warren Barr, is
pretty darn good, too; think creative takes on local produce, including a
bounty of seafood including the freshest crab and halibut."
NATHAN LUMP, Editor-in-Chief, *Travel + Leisure*

"The thriving culinary scene [in Tofino] ... began when a native,
Charles McDiarmid, opened the Wickaninnish Inn.... The restaurant
continues to be at the top of high-end dining destinations in the area."
SHIVANI VORA, *The New York Times*

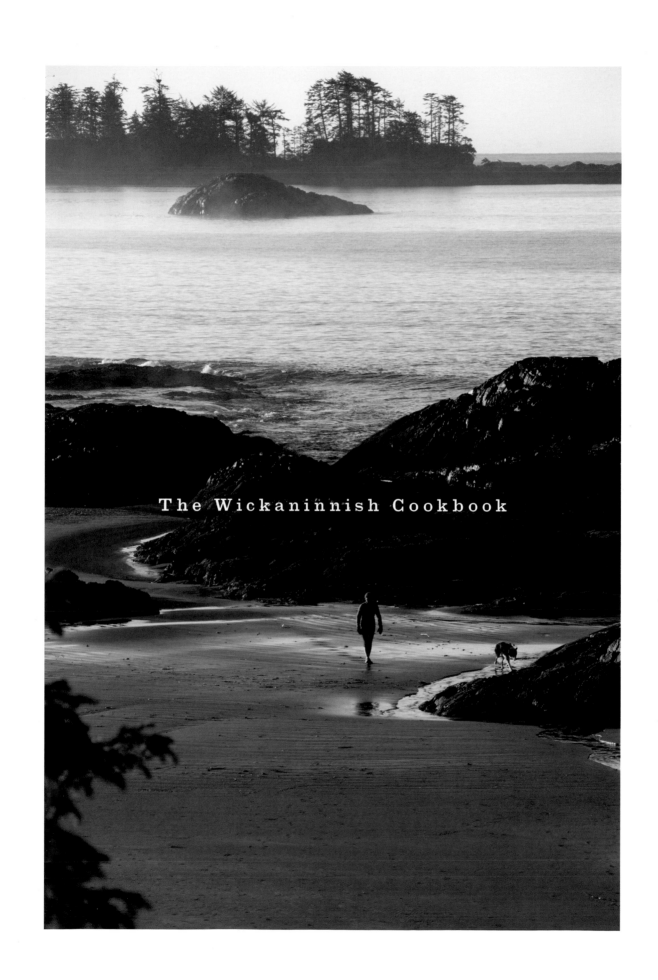

The Wickaninnish Cookbook

the Wick

WRITTEN BY Joanne Sasvari

FOOD PHOTOGRAPHY BY Makito Inomata

RUSTIC ELEGANCE ON NATURE'S EDGE

aninnish
Cookbook

appetite
by RANDOM HOUSE

Contents

List of Recipes

BY THE FIRE: *Casual Fare*

FROM THE SEA: *Seafood*

FROM THE LAND: *Meat, Poultry, and Vegetables*

TO END THE DAY: *Desserts*

ON THE ROCKS: *Wine Cellar and Cocktails*

THE PANTRY: *Vinegars, Oils, Preserves, and More*

WHEN CHARLES McDIARMID invited me to view the site of what would become the Wickaninnish Inn, I'd never set foot in Tofino before. But as we hiked through the forest on our way to that isolated rocky point, overlooking a windswept Chesterman Beach, two realizations struck me: First, I was standing quite literally on the edge of the country (because Tofino is as far west as it gets). And second, I'd need to put my plans to work overseas on hold, because this was the opportunity of a lifetime.

As the opening chef of The Pointe Restaurant, I faced immense challenges. Our remote location required a fair amount of logistical problem solving, including sourcing and transporting food supplies. It also required me to put my growing reputation and influence to work, to convince other chefs that the end of the road was exactly where they needed to be. Additionally, Charles and his family set the bar high—really high. They wanted the world-renowned Relais & Châteaux designation for their beloved Wick, and they wanted me to help get them there.

That fateful journey to the Wick site more than 20 years ago, and the early years I spent at the Inn, have become part of my DNA. I was a determined young chef, and Charles put his faith in me. He knew of my work ethic and my commitment to promoting local ingredients. He knew I'd not only deliver, but I'd go the extra mile to do so, and with his unwavering support, I did. Just a year after opening, we not only had the designation, but we had also earned a reputation within the restaurant community that meant chefs and apprentices no longer needed convincing. The Pointe Restaurant had become a destination, for visitors and staff alike.

And I loved every minute of it. It was an exhilarating, pivotal time in my life, and the fact that the Wick has kept its original dedication to fresh, seasonal, local produce alive gives me a feeling of tremendous accomplishment. The culinary training program I started there has produced a spectacular succession of talented chefs—I ruled with a bit of an iron fist in the early days, so I know they didn't have it easy! Some of those chefs are featured in the pages of this beautiful book.

With the opening of The Pointe Restaurant we kicked off a culinary scene in Tofino that has made that little corner of the world a draw for anyone who appreciates great local food. We built a solid foundation at the Inn, which the very talented Executive Chef Warren Barr, along with Food and Beverage Director Ike Seaman, continue to build on to this day. What the Wick has accomplished has been nothing short of incredible, and I'm so proud to have been a part of it.

CHEF ROD BUTTERS
Opening chef of the Wickaninnish Inn; chef and owner of
RauDZ Creative Concepts, Kelowna, British Columbia

Foreword

THERE'S A MOMENT, when you're driving along Highway 4, after you've passed the stands of towering old-growth Douglas firs of Cathedral Grove and traversed the narrow switchbacks near Kennedy Lake, when you turn a corner, top a rise, and there it is: your first glimpse of the wild west coast of Vancouver Island. A froth of white water rolls onto the wide, sandy strand of Long Beach, where the Pacific Ocean stretches out to meet the horizon.

I've seen this view countless times, and it's nothing short of magical. But for me, it means one thing above all: home.

Just a few minutes farther up the road is the Wickaninnish Inn, the realization of our long-held family dream. Growing up along this wild coast, my parents would talk about opening an inn on the rocks overlooking Chesterman Beach. Our goal was to create a destination that would allow others to discover the remarkable beauty of this part of the world. To have our guests be mesmerized by the rolling waves, meet the fascinating characters we call our neighbours, and revel in the taste of local salmon and crab. We wanted to create a place of quiet serenity right on nature's edge.

"The Wick," as our friends like to call it, has become that place. Today we are a 75-room inn perched on the edge of the Pacific Ocean, with a view of this mighty ocean from every room, suite, and public space. The Inn was the first high-end hotel on the west coast of Vancouver Island and the first destination resort, with all that implies: high-thread-count sheets, attentive service, and a soothing ambience of natural wood, stone, and glass combined with the soft colours of the rainforest. We're honoured to be a member of the Relais & Châteaux family, an international association of intimately scaled luxury properties guided by the five Cs: Calm, Character, Courtesy, Charm, and—perhaps most importantly—Cuisine.

The Pointe Restaurant is the crown jewel of the Wickaninnish Inn. The space is encircled with floor-to-ceiling windows framing a 240-degree panorama of Chesterman Beach, forested offshore islands, and the endless ocean. Inspired by our family cabin on the adjacent point of land, at first glance, the room looks simple: an octagonal space with wooden chairs and tables protected by massive hand-adzed cedar posts and

Introduction

beams fanning out from a central core to the windows and ever-changing vistas beyond. Look closer, though, and you'll see the quiet handcrafted elegance of expertly detailed woodwork and perfectly placed lighting illuminating locally crafted tableware and haunting works by local First Nations artists. We've done all we can to create everything with care, no detail left to chance.

But as spectacular as the scenery is, and as elegant as the décor is, the real masterpieces here are on the plates.

Since opening in 1996, our kitchen has been led by some of Canada's most talented chefs, from our opening chef, Chef Rod Butters, to current Executive Chef Warren Barr. Not only have they prepared delicious meals for our guests, they have also been leaders in the sustainable, seasonal, farm-to-table—or more accurately on this coast, boat-to-table—culinary movement. Long before it was fashionable, they were sourcing produce from the Island's fishers, foragers, and farmers. Through their menus, they celebrated the incredible local seafood bounty, including Dungeness crab, salmon, spot prawns, and halibut, as well as treasures of the forest, such as tender chanterelle mushrooms and tart cynamoka berries. They created a style of cuisine unique to this region; they also inspired other chefs who over time have transformed tiny Tofino into one of Canada's great culinary communities.

In the following pages, we've gathered some of the most unforgettable dishes created by our chefs, including Chef Butters's shellfish-rich potlatch, a West Coast take on bouillabaisse (page 126); Chef Duncan Ly's Thai-scented chowder (page 60); Chef Andrew Springett's cinnamon-scented duck (page 168); Chef Mark Filatow's bright sidestripe prawn escabeche (page 148); Chef Justin Labossiere's saffron-scented ravioli stuffed with crab (page 144); Executive Chef Barr's crispy briny oyster coals (page 130) and his beautifully sculpted salmon mosaic (page 132); Chef Matthias Conradi's decadent chocolate platter for two (page 199); and Chef Matt Wilson's hearty sourdough bread (page 71). There is salmon in a myriad of dishes, crab in almost as many, and chowder, so much chowder.

Are you hungry yet? Well, you're in luck—all the deliciousness of the Wickaninnish Inn lies just ahead. Won't you join us?

CHARLES McDIARMID
Managing Director

THE WEST COAST of Vancouver Island is remote, beautiful, and deceptively serene. For millennia it has been home to the Nuu-chah-nulth First Nations, including the great warrior Chief Wickaninnish, who was leader of the Tla-o-qui-aht band when the Europeans arrived in the 18th century. The expeditions led by Spain's Captain Juan Pérez in 1774 and Britain's Captain James Cook in 1778 were followed by countless explorers seeking treasures of timber, copper, furs, and fish. So great were the potential riches, adventurers happily braved the dangers of a coastline known as the Graveyard of the Pacific, where fog, wind, storms, and waves regularly dashed ships onto jagged rocks or stranded them on hidden sandbars.

Some of those explorers stayed, drawn by the breathtaking beauty and bountiful sea; many of them, no doubt, were happy to make their homes far from the reach of officialdom and familial obligations. Over time, homesteaders, artists, and everyday dreamers settled in alongside their First Nations neighbours. They fished, they logged, they made art, they raised families. And, every once in a while, they welcomed wayward visitors, some of whom never left.

In 1954, a young Dr. Howard McDiarmid stepped off a Queen Charlotte Airlines Canso flying boat and onto a bumpy Second World War airstrip in Tofino. A recent medical school graduate from Winnipeg, he'd been considering a post in even more remote Tahsis. Tofino was only meant to be a stopover on the way back to Vancouver, but it didn't take long for a local delegation to convince him to stay on as the town doctor.

Back then, Tofino had a population of roughly 400 and could be reached only by fishing boat, floatplane, or the aforementioned airstrip. Rugged Ucluelet, 25 miles (40 kilometres) down a rough, muddy road, was twice as big, and the neighbouring First Nations reserves had about as many people as the two villages combined. The hospital was in Tofino, though, so that's where Howard went to work. Initially he signed on for six months, but after falling in love with the place and its people, he ended up settling in for decades and maintaining a home in the area until he passed away in 2010.

At medical school, he'd met a nurse named Lynn Honeyman, who was now working in sunny Bermuda. He wrote her to say that a "friend" would be coming to visit Bermuda and would she mind showing him around? Of course she could, she replied. A few days later, Howard himself turned up, and on June 24, 1955, they were married in Hamilton, Bermuda; shortly thereafter, he convinced her to come back with him to Tofino.

Together, they worked at the Tofino hospital, saving lives and bringing new ones into the world. They had a family of three sons—the Inn's future founder and Managing Director, Charles, and his brothers Jim and Bruce—a daughter, Karen, who died tragically young, as well as a dog named Tigger, several cats, and countless loyal friends. They

History
of the
Wickaninnish
Inn

always lived within view of the ocean. Year after year, they picnicked at a spot on Shell Beach, where they would dream of building a cabin and opening an inn on nearby Chesterman Beach.

In 1959, a logging road was put through from Port Alberni to Tofino. It was a bone-jarring, four-hour trip noted for its vast potholes, terrifying switchbacks, and massive logging trucks loaded with timber. Even so, the road brought more and more people to Tofino. In the 1960s, surfers, draft dodgers, and hippies could be found camping out at Florencia Bay and Schooner Cove. People would drive their vehicles right out onto the pristine sands of Long Beach to camp, dig for razor clams, and enjoy this special oceanside location. Meanwhile, not far away, mountainsides of old-growth forest were being clear-cut at a rapid pace.

Howard knew the more people discovered this beautiful place, the more others would follow in their footsteps. However, with increased tourism and prosperity came the risk of losing what all those visitors were seeking—natural, unspoiled, wild spaces. He was determined to preserve the fragile beauty of the place he loved before it was too late. In 1966, he was elected a Social Credit member of the BC Legislative Assembly, and his main goal was to have the Long Beach area declared a park. In 1971, the federal government announced the creation of the Pacific Rim National Park Reserve. Just a year later, the logging road from Port Alberni was paved, and tourists began to arrive in serious numbers.

By the 1980s, visitors were surfing at Chesterman Beach, hiking the endless sands of Long Beach, soaking in the steamy waters of Hot Springs Cove, and whale watching with local operators like Jamie's Whaling Station. A handful of motels, cabins, campgrounds, and casual eateries opened to serve them.

Meanwhile, the McDiarmids did build their cabin on Shell Beach, and it became their family retreat. It was rustic, isolated, and cozy, with a fireplace and wood-burning stove for heat and propane lamps for light in the dark and stormy winter months. The family would hike from the cabin to the point, a rocky outcrop overlooking Chesterman Beach. There they'd talk about where exactly they would build their inn and how they would welcome the world to the wild west coast. Howard had been a bellhop at the Banff Springs Hotel to put himself through medical school, and he always said he knew just enough about the hotel business to be dangerous.

Charles shared his passion, and left Tofino to attend Cornell University in upstate New York to study the hotel business. He then worked for many years at hotel properties all over North America, mostly for Four Seasons Hotels and Resorts. But he never forgot the dream he and his family shared of opening their own inn. So slowly he started making his way back west, first to Seattle, then to Vancouver, and finally back to Tofino to open the Wickaninnish Inn in 1996. It took the McDiarmids 40 years, but their dream property was built just where it had always been envisioned: on the rocky outcrop at the north end of Chesterman Beach.

OUR GOAL WITH the Inn has always been to create a seamless transition between the natural environment outside and the building's design inside. To do this we use many generously sized and well-positioned windows, and a variety of textured materials and indigenous elements, such as wood and stone. Local artisanship is celebrated throughout the Inn, with handwoven linens, customized furnishings, and carefully placed signature art pieces. Among them are Mark Hobson's mesmerizing seascapes, the haunting works of Roy Henry Vickers, and the delicately carved yellow cedar feathers by Feather George Yearsley. Even the dishes in The Pointe Restaurant are created by a local artist, ceramicist Daniela Petosa. Most significantly, perhaps, master carver Henry Nolla carved the swooping double eagle on the Inn's yellow cedar front doors and hand-adzed the interior posts and beams used throughout the Inn with traditional First Nations tools (a detail you can see on page xiv, and feel replicated on the cover of this book). Today, the tradition of Henry's carving shed continues with master carvers busy at work, and always welcoming to visitors. The Pointe Restaurant's design is based on the McDiarmids' family cabin, a cozy, welcoming space with a convivial fireplace in the middle.

Over the years, the Inn has been recognized with accolades, such as being named a 1997 Grand Award winner in Andrew Harper's *Hideaway Report*, a "connoisseur's worldwide guide to peaceful and unspoiled places," and as the #1 Hotel in North America in *Travel + Leisure*'s 2002 World's Best Awards; as well as receipt of Relais & Châteaux's 2005 Lounge Bar Trophy; recognition for the Ancient Cedars Spa as #1 Resort Spa Overall in *Travel + Leisure*'s 2008 World's Best Awards; and another top Canadian resort rating by *Travel + Leisure* in 2015. What we are most proud of, however, are the longevity Hall of Fame and Platinum awards from *Travel + Leisure* and *Condé Nast Traveler*, consistently naming the Inn as one of the top resorts in Canada year after year for more than 20 years.

The Wickaninnish Inn has inspired several other resorts and hotels to open along the west coast of Vancouver Island. We have turned storm watching into an attraction. We have worked with local operators to turn wildlife viewing, outdoor excursions, artisanship, and foraging into tourism opportunities. But perhaps most of all, we have set the table for our guests to enjoy what we hope is an unforgettable dining experience—with old-growth forest as the backdrop and the surf, sand, islands, and crashing waves of the Pacific Ocean out front and centre.

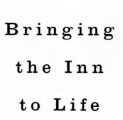

Bringing
the Inn
to Life

Local ceramics artist, Daniela Petosa

Craftsman, "Feather" George Yearsley

TODAY, TOFINO IS a food lover's destination. Visitors plan
their stay not just by what they will see and do, but where they are going
to eat and what they are going to taste. That could be the spicy gumbo
and fried oysters at Wildside Grill, crisp fish tacos and tangy margaritas
at SoBo, or the truffles filled with wild blackberry ganache at Chocolate
Tofino. It could be tender sockeye salmon nigiri or luxuriously rich
shellfish chowder. It will almost certainly include Dungeness crab,
plucked fresh from the waters of Clayoquot Sound and prepared in a
myriad of ways—perhaps baked with cream, or tucked inside a soft
buttered roll, or mounded on top of asparagus and lavished with
hollandaise.

But Tofino wasn't always this way.

Not so long ago, diners who white-knuckled their way along
Highway 4 from Port Alberni to Tofino had two choices: fish 'n' chips at
the Schooner or boiled Dungeness crab at the Crab Bar, where the only
decision was whether to have a whole or half crab. The Crab Bar is now
the casually excellent fine-dining spot Shelter, and after nearly 60 years,
the Schooner is still serving its legendary Admiral's Plate, a cornucopia
of west coast seafood specialities.

The Schooner is a Tofino institution, but it's no longer the only
choice in town. In fact, some days it seems there is a restaurant for every
single one of the approximately 2,000 Tofitians who live here. That
includes two restaurants that have made the prestigious *enRoute* magazine
list of best new restaurants in Canada: SoBo in 2003, when it was still
just a food truck parked in the Tofino Botanical Gardens, and Wolf in
the Fog in 2014. There is Thai, Japanese, and Mexican food, Asian
noodles and Jamaican roti, pizza and burgers, and, of course, endless
bowls of chowder. There is a weekly market in summer, and not one, but
three annual food festivals (Feast Tofino in May, Tofino Food and Wine
Festival in June, and the Clayoquot Oysterfest in November), as well as
the Chowder Chowdown held each March in Ucluelet. Most of all, there
is a strong regional culinary tradition—call it West Coast Island
cuisine—that could only come from this special place on earth.

Since its opening, the Wickaninnish Inn's flagship restaurant, The
Pointe, has established a tradition of celebrating the best of locally fished,

At an

Ocean Table

farmed, and foraged ingredients, prepared with passion and finesse. When Chef Butters opened The Pointe in 1996, he was determined it would go well beyond the chowders and fish 'n' chips that were on most Vancouver Island menus. The Inn would be the only serious fine-dining restaurant on the island north of Victoria, and the only one, aside from Sooke Harbour House, to source most of its own ingredients locally. Back then, most Vancouver Island restaurants received just about everything, from bread to salad dressing to meat, from restaurant supply trucks that came to the coast on a weekly basis. Chef Butters decided The Pointe would be different.

"When we opened, one thing I was dead set on was we'd do everything, absolutely everything, in house," Chef Butters says. He went so far as having the pastry chef whip up a batch of housemade brittle each night to accompany bills as they were going out. "I'm pretty proud of that."

He developed a network of suppliers the Inn still uses today, building relationships with local farmers, fishers, and foragers and creating a market for them where none had existed before. "That was key from the very beginning," Charles recalls. "I think the response at first was somewhat skeptical. But we did what we'd said we would do. If the foragers brought us a good product, and it was at a decent price, Rod would buy it."

> "The Pointe was busy from the moment its doors opened. By setting such a high standard from the start, we were able to attract serious talent despite the remote location."

It turned out what our Inn was serving was exactly what everyone was hungry for. The Pointe was busy from the moment its doors opened. By setting such a high standard from the start, we were able to attract serious talent despite the remote location. Many of the chefs who've been through The Pointe's kitchen have gone on to open their own restaurants and reap their own accolades. They've spread the culture of the Inn far and wide. Chef Butters departed in 1999 to travel the world and ended up in the Okanagan Valley, where he, along with fellow Wickaninnish alum Chef Filatow, is defining BC's wine-country cuisine. After his stint at the Inn, Chef Springett led the kitchen at Black Rock Oceanfront Resort in Ucluelet for years, bringing another fine-dining experience to the village once known only for pub fare. Chef Conradi turned his talents to keeping southern Vancouver Island happy with luxurious patisserie. Chef Ly, Chef Labossiere, and Chef Wilson found themselves in Calgary, carrying the Wick's ideals across the Rockies.

Each chef brought his own vision to the Inn, too. That includes Executive Chef Barr, who honed his farm-to-table skills on Canada's east coast at Prince Edward Island's Inn at Bay Fortune. He joined the Inn in 2011 and has been executive chef since 2013. In that time he has crafted an experience designed to define and elevate Canadian cuisine, offering something unique, and uniquely local.

"My vision for cuisine at the Inn depends on what goggles I am wearing," Executive Chef Barr says. "Every restaurant, and even time of day, has its own purpose as far as catering to our guests' needs." The Driftwood Café, for instance, is a coffee shop in the morning and a cozy spot for comfort food and a glass of wine at night, while On the Rocks Bar & Lounge is ideal for settling in and enjoying a local beer or cocktail with a burger. "The Pointe Restaurant is where we try to offer something more refined and experiential. Our brunch menu walks a tightrope of familiar favourites with just enough finesse or 'pop' to make the meals memorable. At nighttime, we try to take our guests on a bit of a journey and work with more conceptual ideals."

Just as Chef Butters intended more than two decades ago, Executive Chef Barr's team makes everything in house, from crispy baguettes and house churned butter to sausages and ginger beer. It helps that he has access to so many exceptional local ingredients: sablefish and salmon, gooseneck barnacles, oysters, spot prawns, mushrooms, berries, and so much more.

"The access we have to fantastic ingredients is a huge bonus. Not just the Inn, but the town of Tofino is very committed to eating sustainable, island-grown product. This means smaller farmers and businesses are supported enough that they don't need to compromise on what they grow or provide," Executive Chef Barr says. "I think working in a very popular destination town coupled with being part of the Relais & Châteaux family allows us to develop something unique and exciting."

Incredible ingredients, talented chefs, spectacular scenery, stylish comfort, and attentive hospitality—the Wickaninnish Inn is a perfect place to spend a perfect day, and Executive Chef Barr has a good idea of just how that day should unfold.

"I would like every guest to start their day with brunch at The Pointe Restaurant, then take a flaky pastry from the Driftwood Café for a walk on the beach," he says. "Enjoy the Ancient Cedars Spa in the afternoon, topped off with a smoked salmon plate and a glass of bubbles in On the Rocks. Perhaps treat themselves to a nap listening to the waves crash outside. Then come back to The Pointe for a Feather George cocktail and tasting menu in the evening. If every one of our guests had at least one day like that, I would be thrilled."

Why not start right here? What follows is a time capsule of some of our chefs' most popular dishes since 1996, a taste of the Wickaninnish Inn for you to bring home.

"Just as Chef Butters intended more than two decades ago, Executive Chef Barr's team makes everything in house, from crispy baguettes and house churned butter to sausages and ginger beer. It helps that he has access to so many exceptional local ingredients."

(Overleaf) A "room at the inn" for our four-legged friends— Tuktoyaktuk is a regular visitor ▶

A Note on
the Recipes

WHEN WE DECIDED to write this cookbook, we had a big decision to make: Should we feature only the dishes that are currently being served at the Wickaninnish Inn? Or should we offer favourites from the past as well, even if they're no longer on the menu? We quickly realized that this was more than a recipe book. It's the story of a very special place, the people who have helped bring it to life, and the food that has been enjoyed along the way.

So we tracked down many of the chefs who brought their unique flavour to the Inn and gathered two decades of their best-loved dishes in these pages.

Since day one, one of the things that has made dining at the Wickaninnish Inn such a unique culinary experience is the fresh, seasonal, local bounty our chefs can rely on. We also understand home cooks can't necessarily bike over to a nearby dock to pick up a bucket of Dungeness crabs like our apprentices do. So here are a few tips on how to make Inn-style food even if you live far away from the west coast of Vancouver Island.

SEAFOOD: Preferably, buy fish that's fresh and in season. That said, most ocean-caught fin fish is flash-frozen at sea, so you can often find tuna, salmon, and halibut even out of season. More importantly, make sure your seafood is sustainably fished or, yes, farmed—in fact, some farmed seafood, especially shellfish, is more sustainable than wild-caught. Look for labels like Ocean Wise or Seafood Watch. And if you shop at reliable fishmongers, they can tell you about the provenance of whatever you're buying. Please be sure to thoroughly clean all shellfish and remove any opened shells before cooking.

MEAT AND POULTRY: We choose meat from animals that have been raised and processed with care and compassion. It tastes better, but more importantly, it's just the right thing to do.

PRODUCE: Fresh. Seasonal. Local. Organic when possible. We like to support local farmers; food that is picked at the peak of ripeness and delivered fresh that day just tastes better than produce that has been shipped across continents. Farmers' markets are a good source, but many supermarkets offer a wide range of local and organic products too.

FORAGED FOOD: At the Inn, trusted foragers show up at our back door. For home cooks, it's a little more difficult. Foraging is fun, but comes with risks—many poisonous mushrooms, for instance, look just like edible ones. Even flowers or tree tips that are otherwise edible might have been sprayed with toxic chemicals. If you can, purchase wild edibles from trusted sources; you can often find them online. If you can't, you can substitute supermarket choices instead, although they won't have the intense flavours of wild-foraged. For instance, you can use button mushrooms instead of morels or blueberries instead of cynamoka berries. Also consider using dried and rehydrated mushrooms or frozen berries.

ALSO, UNLESS OTHERWISE NOTED:
Butter is unsalted
Cream is heavy (35% butter fat)
Eggs are large
Flour is all-purpose
Herbs are fresh
Juice is fresh and strained
Milk is whole
Olive oil is extra-virgin
Pepper is cracked black
Salt is kosher
Sugar is granulated

Remember, recipes are guidelines, not rules. Please alter, add, or take away as you see fit to create your own perfect dish.

Fresh. Seasonal. Local. Organic when possible. We like to support local farmers; food that is picked at the peak of ripeness and delivered fresh that day.

To Start the Day

▼

BREAKFAST AND BRUNCH

Surfers appear
from the grey fog,
their ghostly
forms as much a
part of the local
scenery as the
sandpiper foot-
prints and wrack
of kelp in the sand.

MORNINGS ARE MAGICAL on Chesterman Beach. Everything is wrapped in a gauzy blanket of mist. It softens the edges of buildings and cloaks the world in silence, muffling the crash of waves lapping the shore, the cries of eagles in the trees, the distant throb of a boat engine. Some days the mist never really lifts; it just gets lighter and whiter as the day goes on. On others the rising sun gilds it with a diffuse golden glow, a trick of the light unique to this stretch of coastline. Eventually, on all but the stormiest of days, surfers appear from the grey fog, their ghostly forms as much a part of the local scenery as the sandpiper footprints and wrack of kelp in the sand.

Long before the surfers climb into their wetsuits, though, the Inn's bakers have been hard at work. They've been baking bread and filling Danishes, pulling tins of muffins out of the oven, popping trays of scones back in. Breakfast has never been an afterthought meal at the Inn. It's the healthy, hearty fuel that powers guests through long days of whale watching and hiking along endless beaches. It can also be an indulgence, a decadent meal to linger over while watching the world come slowly, gloriously to life outside.

At the same time, the morning meal offers a taste of our local ingredients. Guests can savour preserves made with cynamoka berries from the surrounding forest or eggs benny topped with Dungeness crab from Clayoquot Sound. Sausages are crafted in house, and greens are sourced from a lovely farm in nearby Ucluelet. Even the porridge is unique to this place, made hearty with a selection of ancient grains, then indulgent with spiced honey and poached pears.

Whether a guest is grabbing a muffin to go at the Driftwood Café or indulging in a long, leisurely brunch and an extra pot of coffee at The Pointe, chefs are dishing out the perfect start to another west coast day.

Right from the beginning, we knew breakfast was going to be an important part of our culinary day. But because our guests are often rushing out the door to catch the perfect wave or glorious sunrise, breakfast also had to be easy to grab and go, so Chef Butters whipped up this nourishing and bursting-with-flavour granola. He suggests adding your favourite nuts and dried fruit to make it completely your own. If you like, you can serve it as a parfait with layers of yogurt and fresh fruit, the way the Inn does.

DRIED FRUIT GRANOLA

1 cup (80 g) rolled oats
½ cup (45 g) oat bran
¼ cup (45 g) uncooked quinoa
½ Tbsp (3 g) ground cinnamon
¼ cup (35 g) unsalted sunflower
    seeds
3 Tbsp (20 g) sliced almonds
Pinch of salt
2 Tbsp (30 mL) grapeseed oil
3 Tbsp (45 mL) honey
Finely grated zest of ½ orange
2 cups (300 g) chopped dried
    fruit, any combination of
    peaches, pears, raisins, cherries,
    blueberries, figs, apricots, or
    apples
Milk or yogurt, to serve

**MAKES 4 TO 5 CUPS
(1 TO 1.25 L)**

Preheat the oven to 375°F (190°C). Line a baking sheet with parchment paper or a non-stick silicone liner.

In a large bowl, mix together the oats, oat bran, quinoa, cinnamon, sunflower seeds, almonds, salt, and grapeseed oil.

Spread the mixture evenly on the lined baking sheet. Place in the oven and bake for about 12 minutes or until slightly browned.

Remove from the oven and return to the bowl. Add the honey and orange zest. Mix thoroughly and let cool.

Add the chopped dried fruit and mix together well. Serve with milk or yogurt. Stored in a resealable bag or well-sealed container, the granola will keep in the cupboard for several weeks.

Tofino has no shortage of rainy mornings, and there's no better way to start a damp, grey day than with a bowl of rib-sticking porridge. Executive Chef Barr takes what could be a simple cereal and elevates it with ancient grains, spiced honey, poached pears, berries, and seeds, making it a memorable feast in a bowl. Much of this recipe can be prepared a day ahead, with the finishing touches made the morning of.

ANCIENT GRAIN PORRIDGE

ANCIENT GRAINS

¾ cup (130 g) uncooked red quinoa

¾ cup (130 g) uncooked white quinoa

1 cup (195 g) uncooked amaranth grains

Sea salt

SPICED HONEY

¾ cup (180 mL) honey

2 tsp (10 mL) apple cider vinegar

½ tsp (1 g) ground nutmeg

½ tsp (1 g) ground cinnamon

½ tsp (1 g) ground allspice

POACHED PEARS

4 cups (800 g) sugar

1¾ cups (430 mL) white wine

1 vanilla bean, split

4 cups (1 L) water

Juice of 3 lemons

6 pears

PORRIDGE

2 cups (160 g) rolled oats

4 cups (1 L) milk

2 Tbsp (30 g) butter

2 Tbsp (30 g) brown sugar

Pinch of salt

⅓ cup (45 g) dried cranberries

⅓ cup (55 g) dried blueberries

2 Tbsp (20 g) pumpkin seeds

2 Tbsp (20 g) unsalted sunflower seeds

2 cups (about 300 g) fresh mixed berries

SERVES 6

Precook the ancient grains: In three separate pots and following the package instructions, cook both types of quinoa and the amaranth individually in water until they have doubled in volume. Stir regularly to ensure that the grains do not stick to the pot and that they cook evenly, about 10 minutes for the quinoa and 20 for the amaranth. The grains should absorb all the water and be very tender when finished. If they are still crunchy, add more water as needed and continue to cook.

Once cooked, remove the grains from the heat. Mix them together in a large bowl, season very lightly with sea salt, and set aside until ready to use.

MAKE THE SPICED HONEY: In a small pot, combine all the ingredients and bring to a simmer, stirring, until combined. Remove from the heat and set aside.

POACH THE PEARS: In a pot, combine all the poaching ingredients (except the pears) and bring to a simmer. Peel the pears and use a melon baller to remove the core through the bottom of each pear. Place in the poaching liquid and cover the pot. Simmer at a low temperature for about 30 minutes or until the pears are tender when a knife is passed through them. Place the pot in an ice bath and cool with the pears in it.

MAKE THE PORRIDGE: In a large pot set over medium heat, place the oats, milk, butter, brown sugar, and salt and bring to a simmer, stirring constantly. Once the oats are cooked (about 3 minutes), add the cooked amaranth and quinoa and simmer for another few minutes, stirring regularly. The porridge should be thick and rich at this point; if not, simmer a few minutes longer.

Divide the porridge between six bowls. Cut the poached pear into bite-sized pieces. Frame each bowl of porridge with the dried fruits, fresh berries, and poached pear. Finish with a drizzle of spiced honey.

As a pastry chef, Chef Conradi is no stranger to complex recipes. But this simple breakfast muffin is a perennial favourite. The sour cream gives the muffins a wonderful richness, while antioxidant-rich blueberries pop with freshness. Alternatively, you could skip the blueberries and make this sweetly wholesome with carrots, apples, and a touch of spice.

Blueberry SOUR CREAM MUFFINS

4 cups (500 g) flour

2 cups (400 g) sugar

2 tsp (10 g) baking powder

1 tsp (5 g) baking soda

1 tsp (3 g) salt

3 cups (450 g) fresh or frozen
   blueberries

4 eggs

2 cups (500 mL) sour cream

1 cup (250 mL) vegetable oil

1 tsp (5 mL) vanilla extract

**MAKES 12 LARGE OR
18 REGULAR MUFFINS**

Preheat the oven to 350°F (180°C). Lightly spray a muffin tin with vegetable spray.

In a large bowl, combine the dry ingredients. Add the blueberries and lightly toss together.

In a separate, medium-size bowl, whisk the eggs, then stir in the sour cream, vegetable oil, and vanilla. Whisk together until smooth.

Add the wet ingredients to the dry; using a wooden spoon, gently mix together until just combined.

Portion the batter into the prepared muffin tins and bake for 20 to 25 minutes or until the tops are golden and a wooden skewer inserted into the centre of a muffin comes out clean.

½ tsp (1 g) cinnamon

½ tsp (1 g) nutmeg

2 large carrots, peeled and grated

1 large Granny Smith apple,
   peeled, cored, and grated

⅓ cup (75 g) cream cheese

¼ cup (50 g) sugar, or to taste

¼ cup (36 g) pumpkin seeds, or
   to taste

Apple Carrot Variation

Follow the directions above, but add the cinnamon and nutmeg to the dry ingredients, and replace the blueberries with the grated carrots and apples. After you spoon the batter into the prepared muffin tins, place a generous teaspoonful of cream cheese on top of each muffin, then sprinkle with sugar and pumpkin seeds before baking as above.

Pastry Chef Conradi's Danishes were among the favourite breakfast dishes served at the Inn—crisp and flaky, yet mouthwateringly tender and filled with fresh fruit, creamy custard, or a gooey cinnamon caramel. Best of all, they're easy to make ahead of time and freeze for whenever you need a treat.

DANISH PASTRY

BUTTER BLOCK
½ cup (115 g) butter
⅓ cup (40 g) flour

YEAST DOUGH
4 cups (500 g) flour
1 oz (30 g) instant dry yeast
⅓ cup (60 g) sugar
2 Tbsp (30 g) butter
1 tsp (3 g) salt
1 egg
1½ cups (375 mL) milk
Finely grated zest of 1 lemon
1 tsp (5 mL) vanilla extract

Filling (see recipes below)

EGG WASH
1 egg yolk
1 Tbsp (15 mL) milk
Pinch of salt
Pinch of sugar

**MAKES ABOUT
30 DANISHES**

MAKE THE BUTTER BLOCK: In a stand mixer fitted with a paddle attachment, mix the butter and flour together, then form into a square about ½ inch (1 cm) thick. Chill until it is firm but still pliable enough that it doesn't break when you roll it into the dough.

MAKE THE YEAST DOUGH USING THE "ALL-IN" METHOD: In the stand mixer, using the dough hook, mix all the ingredients together at the same time. Knead in the machine at medium speed for 6 to 7 minutes to develop some gluten. Cover and let rest for 20 minutes in the refrigerator.

Roll out the dough to an area twice as big as the butter block. Cover the butter block with the dough and gently roll out into a long rectangle. Fold like a letter, one-third from each side, so you end up with three layers on top of each other. Conradi calls this the single fold. Chill for 20 minutes.

For the double fold, roll out the chilled dough again into a large rectangle twice as long as it is wide, about 12 by 24 inches (30 by 60 cm) then fold it like a book, one-quarter from each side, so the dough ends meet in the centre on top of the remaining rolled dough. Fold it again like a book; you should have four layers of rolled dough on top of each other.

Chill for 20 minutes, then roll out ¼ inch (6 mm) thick and let rest for 10 minutes. Whisk together the egg wash. Cut and fill the dough with your chosen filling—there are a number of ways to do this, including twists, triangles, kites, rolls, puffs and cushions—making sure to brush the pastry with the egg wash before firmly sealing it shut.

Either bake right away in a preheated 400°F (200°C) oven for about 10 minutes, or wrap the filled Danishes in plastic wrap, place in resealable bags, and freeze until ready to use. If you freeze the unbaked Danishes, thaw them overnight in the fridge and then proof in a warm place until they double in size before baking.

Apple Filling

12 McIntosh apples

5 Granny Smith apples

½ cup (115 g) butter

1 cup (200 g) sugar

¼ cup (60 mL) lemon juice

1 tsp (2 g) ground cinnamon

2 Tbsp (30 mL) rum

½ cup (60 g) chopped roasted
hazelnuts

½ cup (64 g) raisins

**MAKES ENOUGH FOR
ABOUT 15 DANISHES**

Peel and core the apples, and cut one-third of them into small dice.

In a large skillet, melt the butter, then stir in the sugar, lemon juice, and cinnamon. Add the diced apples and poach to the desired consistency. Flambé with the rum and cool down.

Slice the remaining two-thirds of the apples very thinly and mix with the hazelnuts and raisins.

Add the poached, diced apples and mix well. Let the mixture sit at room temperature for 3 hours before using to fill the Danishes.

Crème Pâtissière Filling

1¼ cups (300 mL) milk

Scraped-out seeds of ¼ vanilla
bean

½ tsp (2 g) salt

½ tsp (1 g) finely grated lemon
zest

¼ cup (50 g) sugar

3 egg yolks

¼ cup (30 g) flour

Grand Marnier, finely grated
orange zest, or other flavourings (optional)

**MAKES ENOUGH FOR
ABOUT 15 DANISHES**

In a medium-size saucepan over medium heat, boil the milk with the vanilla bean, salt, lemon zest, and half of the sugar.

In a mixing bowl, whisk together the egg yolks with the remaining sugar and the flour.

Slowly whisk the egg mixture into the milk mixture and bring to a rolling boil while stirring constantly. Cook just until thickened, and do not allow to overcook.

Press through a fine-mesh strainer while hot, then place the bowl into an ice bath to cool down.

If you like, you can add a dash or pinch of flavourings such as Grand Marnier or orange zest at this point.

Cover with plastic wrap placed directly on the custard; this will prevent it from forming a skin. Chill until ready to use in Danishes.

Vienna Hazelnut Filling

In a stand mixer, cream the butter with the sugar and cinnamon until light and fluffy.

In a separate bowl, mix the marzipan with the egg whites, then stir into the butter mixture. Fold in the hazelnuts and incorporate well.

Use at room temperature to fill Danishes.

¾ cup (170 g) butter

2 cups (400 g) sugar

1 tsp (2 g) ground cinnamon

⅜ cup (100 g) marzipan

2 egg whites

2 cups (225 g) roughly chopped hazelnuts

MAKES ENOUGH FOR ABOUT 15 DANISHES

The sweet or savoury soft biscuits known as scones are best enjoyed alongside morning coffee or afternoon tea. The scones at the Inn are a favourite with guests, especially these orange-scented, currant-studded ones.

CURRANT SCONES

3¼ cups (400 g) flour

1 Tbsp + 2 tsp (23 g) baking
    powder

¾ tsp (2 g) salt

⅓ cup (60 g) sugar

Finely grated zest of ½ orange

½ cup (115 g) cold butter, cut into
    small pieces

1 egg

1 cup (250 mL) buttermilk

2 Tbsp (30 mL) honey

1 cup (145 g) dried currants

1 egg yolk

2 Tbsp (30 mL) milk

Icing sugar, for dusting (optional)

**MAKES ABOUT 12
SCONES**

In a large bowl, sift together the flour and baking powder, then whisk in the salt, sugar, and orange zest, making sure they are evenly combined.

Using a pastry blender, cut in the cold butter until the mixture resembles peas. Alternatively, place the flour mixture and butter in a food processor and pulse until it's cut in, being careful not to overprocess.

In a separate bowl, whisk the whole egg with the buttermilk and honey. Form a well in the dry ingredients and, using a wooden spoon, mix in the liquid ingredients.

Fold in the currants, mixing until evenly combined but still a bit crumbly and loose. Do not overwork the dough; it should be just manageable.

Gather the dough into a ball and let it rest for 30 minutes.

Roll the dough into a square 1½ inches (4 cm) thick, and let it rest for another 30 minutes.

Meanwhile, preheat the oven to 325°F (160°C) and line a baking sheet with parchment paper.

Mix the egg yolk and milk together to form an egg wash, then brush it over the surface of the scone dough. Cut into 2-inch (5 cm) squares and bake for 20 minutes or until lightly golden on top and baked through. Dust them with icing sugar to finish. These will keep for two to three days.

Simple but satisfying, this banana bread from Pastry Chef Conradi is one you will want to make again and again. Buttermilk and ground hazelnuts give it richness and depth, elevating it well beyond your ordinary breakfast loaf. It also makes a perfect afternoon snack with a warming mug of hot chocolate.

BANANA BREAD

Butter for loaf pan
2 cups (200 g) pastry flour, plus
    more for loaf pan
2 large bananas
1 Tbsp (15 g) baking soda
1 cup (200 g) sugar
3 eggs
⅓ cup (80 mL) vegetable oil
⅓ cup (80 mL) buttermilk
¾ cup (75 g) ground hazelnuts
Icing sugar, for dusting (optional)

MAKES 1 LOAF

Preheat the oven to 350°F (180°C). Butter and flour one large (9 × 5 × 3-inch/23 × 13 × 8 cm) loaf pan.

Mash the bananas and set aside.

In a large bowl, sift the flour and baking soda, then stir in the sugar.

In a medium-size bowl, whisk together the eggs, vegetable oil, and buttermilk. Stir in the mashed bananas.

Stir the liquid ingredients into the dry ingredients, making sure there are no dry patches of flour remaining. Gently fold in the hazelnuts at the end, but be careful not to overmix.

Scrape into the loaf pan and bake for 45 minutes to 1 hour or until the top is golden and firm and a wooden skewer inserted into the centre comes out clean. Dust with icing sugar to finish.

Even better than eggs Benedict, this beautiful brunch dish from Executive Chef Barr has it all: a crispy potato pancake base, a savoury spinach nest, smoked salmon, poached eggs, and a fragrant hollandaise sauce spooned on top.

SMOKED SALMON ROSTIS

MAKE THE ROSTIS: Boil the whole potatoes in salted water for about 20 minutes or until a knife passes through them with just a little resistance; they should still be a bit firm. Drain the potatoes and cool them completely in the refrigerator. This will take a couple of hours.

Peel the cooled potatoes, then grate using the large holes of a box grater.

Finely chop the green onions and add them to the potatoes. Peel the horseradish and use a zester to grate it into the mix.

Finally, stir together the corn starch and 1½ Tbsp (22 mL) canola oil until well combined, then drizzle it overtop the potato mixture. Season with salt and pepper, then gently mix the rosti together, taking care to keep the grated pieces of potato intact.

When evenly combined, form six large, evenly sized potato pancakes about ½ inch (1.5 cm) thick—use a ring mould if you have one. Cover and place in the fridge until you're ready to cook them.

Preheat the oven to 200°F (95°C).

Using a large non-stick pan and the remaining canola oil, shallow-fry the rostis, about 5 minutes per side, turning only once, until golden and crispy on both sides. Place in the oven to keep warm.

POACH THE EGGS: Bring a large pot of water to a boil and add the white vinegar. Stir the water until it is swirling and has a slight vortex. Carefully crack the eggs into the pot one at a time, taking care not to break the yolks. Cook until the whites are hard but the yolks are still soft, 3 to 5 minutes. Carefully remove eggs from the poaching water and place them on a paper towel.

MAKE THE SPINACH: Meanwhile, in a sauté pan over medium heat, melt the butter and cook the spinach just until it is wilted.

TO ASSEMBLE: Place a rosti in the centre of each of six plates. Top each rosti with a nest of wilted spinach, then divide the salmon between the rosti and place a few slices on top of each mound of spinach. If you like, scoop a spoonful of cream cheese onto each rosti.

Place two eggs in each spinach nest. Top the eggs with hollandaise, then sprinkle with dill, capers, and sliced shallots.

ROSTIS
3 large russet potatoes
2 green onions
1 thumb of fresh horseradish, or about 2 tsp (10 mL) prepared
1½ Tbsp (12 g) corn starch
1 cup (250 mL) canola oil
Salt and cracked black pepper to taste

POACHED EGGS
⅔ cup (160 mL) white vinegar
12 eggs, room temperature

SPINACH
1 Tbsp (15 g) butter
1 lb (450 g) spinach

ASSEMBLY
1 lb (450 g) smoked salmon
¾ cup (170 g) cream cheese (optional)
Hollandaise sauce (recipe follows)
Dill leaves, chopped, to taste
Capers to taste
1 shallot, sliced into thin rings

SERVES 6

Recipe continues ▶

Hollandaise Sauce

½ cup (125 mL) white wine
½ cup (125 mL) white wine vinegar
1 bay leaf
2 sprigs dill, stems only, chopped
1 shallot, sliced
3 egg yolks, room temperature
1½ cups (345 g) butter, melted
  and clarified
Juice of 1 lemon
Salt and cracked black pepper to
  taste

**MAKES ABOUT 2 CUPS
(500 ML)**

Select a small to medium-size pot that will allow a small metal bowl to sit on top. Half fill the pot with water, place it on the stove, and bring the water to a simmer.

In another small pot, place the wine, vinegar, bay leaf, chopped dill stems, and sliced shallots and bring the mixture to a simmer. Simmer until the liquid is reduced by half, then strain out the solids.

In a small metal bowl, place the vinegar reduction and the egg yolks and whisk together. Put the bowl on the small pot of simmering water and whisk vigorously. Continue to whisk until the hollandaise is fluffy and forms soft peaks.

Remove the bowl from the pot and slowly drizzle in the clarified butter, whisking continuously to emulsify the hollandaise. Season with lemon juice, salt, and pepper. Serve immediately.

Executive Chef Barr's hearty, healthy baked eggs are the perfect morning starter for guests who have an energetic day of surfing, hiking, or whale watching ahead. At home, these can also make a satisfyingly savoury light lunch.

BAKED EGGS

MAKE THE TOMATO SAUCE: In a large pot over medium heat, heat the olive oil, then add the shallots and garlic and cook until soft and translucent. Add the tomatoes and season with a generous pinch of salt. Add the thyme and star anise and cover with a sheet of parchment paper (this is known as a cartouche).

Simmer until nearly dry, about an hour, then remove the cartouche, season again with salt, and cook out any remaining liquid. Remove the thyme and the star anise. Season to taste with sherry vinegar.

This can be made a day or so ahead of time. It will likely make more than you need, so freeze whatever is left over or use it in another dish.

MAKE THE BAKED EGGS: Preheat the oven to 350°F (180°C).

In an ovenproof frying pan over medium heat, cook the bacon until crisp and the fat has rendered. Strain the bacon out and set it aside, reserving the bacon fat.

Toss the yam in the remaining bacon fat. Sprinkle with a pinch of salt and place in the oven. Bake until golden and soft, about 20 minutes, then remove from the oven and drain off the excess bacon fat. Turn the oven to broil.

Meanwhile, reheat the tomato sauce if necessary.

Place six small skillets or large ramekins (about 6 oz (170 mL)) on a rimmed baking sheet, and distribute the yam, kale, and bacon evenly between them. Ladle about ½ cup (125 mL) hot tomato sauce into each vessel. Carefully make a little hole in the centre of the tomato sauce in each dish and crack an egg into it.

Place the dishes under the broiler and bake until the egg whites start to become solid white—this could take 5 to 10 minutes. Remove from the oven and grate the Parmesan over each dish. Return to the oven and broil until the egg whites have set and the cheese is golden, another 2–5 minutes.

Slice the baguette into six thick pieces and drizzle with olive oil. Broil until well toasted and serve alongside each baked egg.

TOMATO SAUCE

⅞ cup (200 mL) olive oil

3 shallots, sliced

12 cloves garlic, sliced

5 lb (2.2 kg) tomatoes, peeled, seeded, and diced

Salt to taste

1 sprig thyme

2 pods star anise

Sherry vinegar to taste

BAKED EGGS

7 oz (200 g) double-smoked bacon, diced

1 small yam, peeled and diced

Pinch of salt

2 large leaves kale, thinly sliced

3 cups (750 mL) tomato sauce

6 eggs

3½ oz (90 g) Parmesan cheese

1 baguette

Olive oil

SERVES 6

At the Inn, brunch is always a special occasion, a time to relax, watch the waves, and enjoy some of the best food the chefs can produce, like Executive Chef Barr's rich French toast. Spiced apple butter is tucked inside tender brioche that is battered, fried, and baked, then served with spice-roasted apples. Sweet and delicately spiced, it would star as the centrepiece of any special brunch menu.

Orchard–Stuffed FRENCH TOAST

SPICE-ROASTED APPLES

4 Gala apples
¼ cup (60 g) butter
¼ cup (55 g) brown sugar
½ tsp (1 g) ground cinnamon
½ tsp (1 g) ground allspice
¼ tsp (0.5 g) ground cloves
Juice of 1 lemon

CHANTILLY CREAM

1¼ cups (300 mL) cream
½ tsp (2 mL) vanilla paste or 1 tsp
   (5 mL) vanilla extract
¾ cup (90 g) icing sugar

BATTER

3 eggs
2 egg yolks
2 cups (500 mL) cream
¼ cup (50 g) sugar
Pinch of ground cinnamon

FRENCH TOAST

1 large loaf brioche, cut into
   6 thick, even slices
1 cup (250 mL) apple butter
   (purchased or recipe on
   page 271), plus extra for
   serving
Butter for frying

SERVES 6

Preheat the oven to 350°F (180°C) and place a large baking dish in the oven to warm.

MAKE THE SPICE-ROASTED APPLES: Peel the apples and remove the cores. Slice each apple in half, then slice each half into four wedges (eight wedges per apple).

   In a wide frying pan, melt the butter and brown sugar with the spices, stirring well. When the brown sugar is melted and starts to caramelize, add the apples and toss until evenly coated in caramel and butter. Cook until the apples are tender, about 5 minutes, then finish with a little lemon juice.

MAKE THE CHANTILLY CREAM: Whip the cream until soft peaks form, then add the vanilla and sift in the icing sugar. Continue to beat until stiff peaks form. Chill until ready to use.

MAKE THE BATTER: Whisk together the eggs, egg yolks, cream, sugar, and cinnamon.

MAKE THE FRENCH TOAST: Make a deep incision in the side of each slice of brioche to form a deep pocket. Fill the pocket with as much apple butter as possible without it overflowing. Soak each brioche slice in the batter for 5 minutes; don't leave it too long, or it will get soggy.

   Heat a wide frying pan over medium heat and add a couple of tablespoons of butter. When the butter has melted, fry each slice of stuffed brioche in the butter, adding more butter if needed, until it is golden on each side. Place in the warm baking dish in the oven to finish, baking for about 15 minutes or until slightly puffy and firm to the touch.

   Place a slice of French toast on each of six plates and garnish with the spice-roasted apples, Chantilly cream, and a generous dollop of apple butter.

Granola isn't just for breakfast. Executive Chef Barr's sweet and nutty granola bars make a satisfying snack to enjoy on a hike along the beach or tucked into a lunch bag. Be sure to press these very firmly into the pan or they are likely to crumble.

GRANOLA BARS

4 cups (320 g) rolled oats

1 cup (115 g) sliced almonds

⅔ cup (95 g) unsalted sunflower
　　seeds

⅓ cup (45 g) flaxseeds

¾ cup (45 g) wheat germ

1⅛ cups (280 mL) honey

⅓ cup (75 g) brown sugar

1 cup (145 g) pitted and chopped
　　dates

1 cup (250 mL) water

1½ cups (190 g) dried fruit such
　　as cranberries or raisins

6 oz (170 g) milk or dark
　　chocolate (optional)

MAKES 24 TO 30 BARS

Preheat the oven to 300°F (150°C). Line a rimmed baking sheet (13 × 18 inches/33 × 45 cm) with aluminum foil or parchment paper, making sure to leave enough overhang so it will be easy to lift the bars out of the pan later. Set aside.

Mix the oats, almonds, sunflower seeds, flaxseeds, and wheat germ together and spread evenly on another rimmed baking sheet. Place in the oven and toast until fragrant and lightly golden, 30 to 45 minutes. Do not allow to burn.

In a saucepan, place the honey, brown sugar, chopped dates, and water and bring to a boil. Simmer for a few minutes until the dates are soft and starting to fall apart.

Pour the warm dry ingredients into a large bowl and mix in the hot liquid ingredients, stirring until well blended. Add the dried fruit, mixing thoroughly. Scrape the granola mixture onto the prepared baking sheet and press firmly and evenly into the pan. Be careful; it will still be hot. It's easier to make the mixture even if you take another baking sheet and press it on top. Set aside to cool.

Once cool, cut into bars of whatever size you desire. If you like, melt the chocolate and spread on top of the bars, then place them on a rack to allow the chocolate to set. Store the granola bars in the fridge; they will keep for several weeks.

"The access to seafood was incredible. Oysters. Dungeness crab. Salmon. You could hardly handle these things, they were so fresh. How can you beat that?"

BY 1996, ROD BUTTERS was looking for a new challenge. He had been cooking at the Pacific Palisades Hotel in Vancouver, and was considering making a move to Asia. Luckily, he heard that Charles was planning to open an inn in Tofino. They'd need a chef, Charles said. Asia, it seemed, could wait a while.

Chef Butters and his business partner Audrey Surrao, who would take care of special events, joined Charles on a scouting trip to Tofino. "I'd never been to Tofino in my entire life. It was beautiful blue sky, which I would joke was probably the last time it was sunny in Tofino. How could you not fall in love with the place? And it was closer than Asia," Chef Butters recalls with a laugh. "It was really decided that day, sitting at the family cabin, looking at Chesterman Beach and being part of something new."

Charles essentially gave his new chef de cuisine carte blanche, saying only that he wanted to highlight the local seafood. Perfect, thought Chef Butters, who even in Vancouver was sourcing fresh, local ingredients long before it became fashionable. Chef Butters immediately decided to serve as much local fare as possible and to make as much as he could in-house.

"When you have the best seafood, it's easy not to mess around with it," he says. "The access to seafood was incredible. Oysters. Dungeness crab. Salmon. You could hardly handle these things, they were so fresh. We had a crab boat by the marina and we'd send the young apprentice down every day to bring whatever crab we needed that night for service. How can you beat that?"

After three years, though, Chef Butters says, "I was tired and needed to recharge." For 16 months, he and Audrey travelled around the world, and when they returned they began looking at the Okanagan Valley. In 2001, they opened Fresco, which would come to define wine-country cooking just as The Pointe did coastal cuisine. They rebranded it RauDZ Regional Table in 2009, and then in 2014, they opened micro bar • bites. In 2017, Chef Butters published his first cookbook, *The Okanagan Table*, and the duo launched yet another venture, Terrafina at Hester Creek by RauDZ.

But even now, he looks back fondly at his time at the Inn. "Those were pretty phenomenal days," he says. "I worked my absolute butt off while I was there. When I look at what we accomplished with the people we had, it's just incredible."

◀ *Chef Butters's Potlach (recipe on page 126)*

Storm Watching

▼

SOUPS AND BREADS

"From November through March, an average of 330 to nearly 500 millimetres (13 to 19 inches) of rain falls each month on Vancouver Island's west coast. Gore-Tex is a must. So are rubber boots, a good hat, and a sense of humour."

GREY CLOUDS MASS overhead, dark and dramatic, swollen with rain. Wind sweeps across the sands of Chesterman Beach, sending cedar and spruce branches tossing wildly. Waves crash on the rocks below The Pointe building, racing up the surge channel, spume hurtling into the air. Rain lashes the windows, rat-a-tat-tatting loudly. Lights flicker and fade. Suddenly, candlelight is not just romantic, but a necessity.

From November through March, an average of 330 to nearly 500 millimetres (13 to 19 inches) of rain falls each month on Vancouver Island's west coast. Gore-Tex is a must. So are rubber boots, a good hat, and a sense of humour.

Growing up on this wild shore, Charles loved storm season. He loved gathering with family around the fireplace in his parents' home, listening to the rain hammer on the roof and the wind howl 'round the eaves, safe and warm and well fed inside while the elements raged outside. He figured other people would love it, too.

Incorporating the storm watching experience for our guests was part of the plan from the very beginning. In fact, the entire design of the Inn was built around the concept. Custom storm watching packages are offered November through February, promoting the high winds and plentiful downpours. Some scoff, but others grab their rain gear and head for the tempestuous coast. Now storm watching has become synonymous with Tofino and a season to celebrate.

It's also the season for heartwarming soups and stews or chowders chunky with clams and oysters, best enjoyed with hearty breads slathered in butter and a pint of ale to quench the thirst.

Chowder, that classic cauldron of seafood and vegetables simmered in cream or broth, travelled to these shores from Brittany by way of England, brought long ago by ex-pat loggers, sailors, miners, and explorers. Even before The Pointe Restaurant opened in 1996, visitors to Tofino could be sure of a good bowl of chowder at the end of the long potholed logging road from Port Alberni. It would be hot and rich, thick with clams, bacon, potatoes, and cream. But it took The Pointe to elevate chowder to the extraordinary.

Depending on the season, the Inn's chowders, seafood stews, and other soups might feature clams, oysters, spot prawns, scallops, salmon, ling cod, sablefish, a dash of squid ink for drama, and perhaps even a crab claw or two. They might have the aroma of wood fire from hunks of smoked salmon, the delicate fragrance of dill or tarragon, even the exotic perfume of Asian spices: lemongrass, chilies, curry, coconut milk.

In the following pages, you'll find some of the Inn's most popular chowders, soups, and stews, along with breads to sop up every last delicious drop. They're just what you crave whenever the wind howls and the rain pours.

Rich, creamy, and loaded with local seafood, Chef Labossiere's classic west coast seafood chowder is the perfect meal for a cold and stormy night, especially if you serve it with rustic bread and a pint of beer. Expect your guests to demand seconds.

West Coast SEAFOOD CHOWDER

In a large pot with a lid, bring the stock to a boil. Add the mussels, cover, and steam until the shells open, 4 to 5 minutes.

Remove the mussels from the liquid and allow to cool slightly. Discard any mussels that have not opened. Strain the liquid, cover, and refrigerate until ready to use. Remove the mussel meat from the shells, cover, and refrigerate until ready to use. If you like, you can set aside a few in the shell for garnish.

Rinse out and dry the pot and return it to the stove. Add the bacon and cook over medium heat until crisp. Remove the bacon, leaving the fat in the pot, and dry on a paper towel.

Add the butter to the bacon fat and heat until foamy. Add the diced onions, fennel, and celery; cook until soft and translucent, 8 to 10 minutes, stirring occasionally. Season with sea salt.

Meanwhile, in a medium-size saucepan, place the milk and cream and cook over medium heat, but do not allow to boil.

Stir the flour into the vegetables and cook, stirring, until thickened—this will create a liaison and prevent the chunky bits of vegetable and seafood from sinking to the bottom of your bowl later.

Pour the hot milk mixture slowly into the vegetables, stirring constantly until well blended and smooth. Bring back to a simmer, stirring frequently.

Stir in the potatoes, bacon, and reserved cooking liquid from the mussels. Return to a simmer and cook until the potatoes are tender, 15 to 20 minutes.

Add the cooked mussels, chopped oyster meat, and cubed fish and cook for 4 to 5 minutes, stirring occasionally. Season with salt and pepper and, if you like, a few dashes of hot sauce and/or Worcestershire sauce.

1 cup (250 mL) chicken or fish stock

2 lb (900 g) Salt Spring Island mussels, rinsed well in cold water, any opened shells discarded

6 to 7 oz (175 to 200 g) good-quality bacon, diced

6 Tbsp (85 g) butter

1 large yellow onion, finely diced

½ medium bulb fennel, finely diced

2 medium stalks celery, finely diced

Sea salt and cracked black pepper to taste

6 cups (1.5 L) milk

2 cups (500 mL) cream

½ cup (65 g) flour

3 medium yellow-fleshed potatoes, unpeeled, diced small

½ lb (225 g) oyster meat (or 12 beach oysters, shucked), roughly chopped

1 lb (450 g) fresh halibut or cod, cubed

Tabasco or other hot sauce (optional)

Worcestershire sauce (optional)

SERVES 4 TO 8

2 Tbsp (30 g) butter

2 stalks lemongrass, cut into 2 or
    3 pieces and lightly smashed

1 small bulb ginger, about
    2 inches (5 cm), peeled and
    roughly chopped

1 large carrot, roughly chopped

4 stalks celery, roughly chopped

1 large yellow onion, roughly
    chopped

1 leek, white part only, thinly
    sliced

4 cloves garlic, roughly chopped

2 lb (900 g) kuri squash, peeled,
    seeded, and cut into 1-inch
    (2.5 cm) cubes

8 cups (2 L) chicken stock

8 cups (2 L) coconut milk

1 to 2 Tbsp (15 to 30 mL) Thai red
    curry paste

Juice of 3 limes

1 Tbsp (15 mL) fish sauce

Salt and white pepper to taste

CHOWDER

2 cups (230 g) diced kuri squash

2 cups (300 g) diced potatoes

8 baby squash (pattypan or
    crookneck), quartered

4 small kohlrabi, peeled and
    quartered

½ cup (65 g) pearl onions

1 to 1½ lb (450 to 675 g) spot
    prawns

1 to 1½ lb (450 to 675 g) mussels

1 to 1½ lb (450 to 675 g) halibut,
    cut into 1-inch (2.5 cm) dice

2 cups (500 mL) whipping cream

Chives or cilantro, chopped, for
    garnish

Olive oil, for garnish

SERVES 8

Chowder on this coast is typically rich and creamy, perhaps scented with dill or tarragon. Sometimes it's tomato-based, with the savoury flavours of the Mediterranean. But Chef Ly looked to his Asian heritage to create a chowder that is bright and vibrant with the flavours of ginger, lemongrass, and Thai curry. This chowder is made hearty with two kinds of squash as well as a variety of west coast seafood.

Kuri SQUASH and SEAFOOD CHOWDER

MAKE THE CHOWDER BASE: In a large stockpot over medium heat, melt the butter. Add the lemongrass, ginger, carrots, celery, onions, leek, and garlic. Turn the heat down to low. Slowly sweat the vegetables for 15 to 20 minutes or until they are tender. Then add the squash and continue cooking for approximately 10 minutes.

Add the chicken stock to the pot. Bring to a boil, then lower the heat and simmer for about 10 minutes. Add the coconut milk and red curry paste and continue to simmer for about 15 minutes.

Remove the lemongrass stalks, then, using a blender, process the chowder base until smooth and creamy. Strain the chowder base through a fine-mesh strainer and add the lime juice and fish sauce. Season with salt and white pepper to taste.

MAKE THE CHOWDER: First, in a large pot, bring the chowder base to a boil. Add the diced squash, potatoes, baby squash, kohlrabi, and pearl onions and cook until tender, approximately 15 minutes.

Add the prawns, mussels, and halibut and cook until the mussels open and the seafood is cooked, about a minute or two. Discard any shells that do not open. Stir in the cream and cook for 1 minute.

Serve the chowder in bowls topped with chopped chives or cilantro and a drizzle of olive oil.

About three weeks after the Inn opened, Chef Filatow was promoted to his second position in the kitchen; as entremetier, he was responsible for soups, vegetables, and egg dishes. "Every morning I would start my day with making 25 litres of chowder," he recalls. "It had to be different than the day before. I made it for the evening service and lunch service the next day. After a year of this, it was safe to say I had made some soup. This is one of my favourites."

SABLEFISH, CLAM, POTATO, and BACON CHOWDER

In a medium-size pot, bring the white wine to a simmer and reduce by half.

Rinse the clams under cold water, then add to the pot. Cover with a tight-fitting lid and slowly cook until the clams open. (This should take only a few minutes.) Remove the clams, reserving the liquid, and refrigerate both until cool. Discard any shells that do not open.

Place a pot big enough to accommodate 12 cups (3 L) on medium heat. Add the butter and bacon. Once the bacon is sizzling, add the onions, carrots, and garlic. Cook until the onions are translucent. Add the potatoes and stir them around for 1 minute.

Add the stock, cream, and cooking liquid from the clams. Cook on a low simmer until the potatoes are just cooked through, about 15 to 20 minutes.

Remove from the heat. Ladle about 2 cups (500 mL) of the soup, including the chunky ingredients, into a blender. Purée until smooth, taking care not to splatter the hot soup.

Return the puréed soup to the pot. Check for seasoning and add salt and pepper to taste. If not using the soup right away, chill down in an ice bath before placing in the fridge.

To finish, heat the soup slowly to a simmer. Right before serving, add the sablefish and cooked clams. Season with salt and pepper and finish with a little chopped parsley or tarragon and/or lemon juice if desired. Ladle into soup plates and enjoy!

½ cup (125 mL) crisp white wine
1 lb (450 g) littleneck clams in shell
7 Tbsp (100 g) butter
¼ lb (110 g) bacon, diced
1 small onion, diced small
1 medium carrot, peeled and diced small
2 small cloves garlic, finely chopped
3 medium yellow-fleshed potatoes, peeled and diced in ½-inch (1 cm) cubes
4 cups (1 L) chicken stock or good-quality fish stock
2 cups (500 mL) whipping cream
Salt and cracked black pepper
½ lb (225 g) sablefish, cut into bite-size pieces
Chopped flat-leaf parsley, chopped tarragon, and/or lemon juice (optional)

SERVES 4 TO 6

Photo on page 74

CLAM and CORN CHOWDER

1 lb (450 g) clams in shell

½ cup (125 mL) white wine

1 medium onion, diced

1 bulb fennel, diced

1 stalk celery, diced

2 Yukon gold potatoes, peeled and
    diced

Canola or vegetable oil

1 strip bacon, chopped

2 Tbsp (15 g) flour

1½ cups (375 mL) chicken stock

1 ear corn, kernels only

½ lb (225 g) fresh white fish,
    cubed

½ lb (225 g) baby shrimp or any
    other seafood

Juice of 1 lemon

Salt and cracked black pepper to
    taste

1 cup (250 mL) cream

Herbs (dill, chives, flat-leaf
    parsley), chopped, for garnish

SERVES 4

In a large pot, place the clams, white wine, and 1 Tbsp (15 mL) each of chopped onions, fennel, and celery. Cover and steam until the clams open, 5 to 10 minutes.

Strain the juice from the pan and reserve. Remove the clams from their shells and save the meat; chill until ready to use. Discard the shells and vegetables, as well as any clams that do not open.

Meanwhile, cook the peeled and diced potatoes in salted water until tender, about 10 minutes. Drain off the water and reserve the potatoes.

Heat a large pot over medium heat, then add a splash of oil and the chopped bacon. Cook on medium until the bacon has a rich colour and the fat has rendered out. Add the remaining chopped onions, fennel, and celery and cook until tender.

Add the flour and stir to prevent it from sticking to the pot. Cook for a couple of minutes, but do not allow to brown—you want the roux to be white.

Stir in the reserved clam juice and cook until thick. Stir in the chicken stock and cook until slightly less thick.

Add the corn and cook until tender—this should take only a couple of minutes. Add the clam meat, cubed white fish, and any other seafood. Finally, add the potatoes and heat through. Season with lemon juice, salt, and pepper, then stir in the cream. Garnish each serving with herbs.

When the Inn first opened, there were two dishes everyone talked about: Chef Butters's potlatch and his crab cappuccino. Essentially a fragrant crab bisque topped with a cloud of steamed milk, the latter made the most of one of the region's greatest ingredients—Dungeness crab—while offering a sophisticated take on a local favourite, chowder. Chef Butters suggests pairing it with the crisp, minerally Road 13 Vineyards 2015 Chip off the Old Block Chenin Blanc from Oliver.

CRAB CAPPUCCINO

2 small whole crabs, cooked

¼ cup (60 mL) grapeseed oil

¼ cup (60 g) butter

1 small onion, diced

1 stalk celery, diced

¼ bulb fennel, diced

8 mushrooms, sliced

3 cloves garlic, chopped

¼ cup (60 mL) tomato paste

¼ cup (30 g) flour

6 cups (1.5 L) vegetable stock

1 cup (250 mL) cream

1 cup (240 g) canned diced
   tomatoes

1 tsp (3 g) black peppercorns

1 tsp (2 g) fennel seeds

1 tsp (2 g) mustard seeds

4 bay leaves

Sea salt and cracked black pepper
   to taste

1 cup (250 mL) milk

Fennel fronds, for garnish
   (optional)

SERVES 4

Photo on page 83

Remove the crabmeat from the shells and set aside. Break the crab shells into small pieces.

Heat a large pot on medium-high heat. Add the oil and the crab shells. Cook until the shells start to take on some caramelized colour, 7 to 10 minutes.

Stir in the butter until melted, then add the onions, celery, fennel, mushrooms, and garlic. Continue cooking and stirring until the bottom of the pot starts to colour and the vegetables are soft and starting to caramelize.

Add the tomato paste and continue cooking. The bottom of the pot should now be taking on a lot of colour. Stir, scraping the bottom of the pot, for 3 to 5 minutes, until the vegetables are quite caramelized.

Add the flour and stir thoroughly. Cook for 1 minute. Add the stock, cream, tomatoes, peppercorns, seeds, and bay leaves. Mix well, making sure the bottom of the pot is scraped clean as much as possible.

Reduce the heat to a low simmer, cover the pot partially with a lid, and cook for 35 to 45 minutes, stirring occasionally. Remove from the heat and strain carefully through a fine-mesh strainer, discarding the solids. Strain again, making sure the soup is silky smooth. Season to taste with salt and pepper.

You can prepare the soup base a day ahead to this point; chill until ready to serve.

To serve: Heat the soup to a simmer. Divide the crabmeat between four large cappuccino cups or latte bowls. Ladle the soup on top.

Using a cappuccino machine, steam the milk, then spoon on top of the crab soup. (Alternatively you can heat the milk in a small pot and whisk it to create a foamy froth on top.) If you like, garnish with fennel fronds.

For Chef Labossiere, this is a staple when having friends over. He likes to serve the Indian-inspired flatbread with dips or spreads or even smoked fish and pickles. He makes it with fresh yeast, also known as cake yeast, which can be hard to find. You can use active dry yeast instead; just follow the proportions below.

NAAN-STYLE BREAD

In a small saucepan, combine the butter, cream, and milk. Gently warm until the butter is melted, stirring frequently.

In the bowl of a stand mixer fitted with a dough hook, combine the flour, sugar, salt, and baking powder.

If you are using fresh yeast, in a small bowl, whisk together the yeast, egg yolk, and water. If you are using dry yeast, dissolve it in the warm water, then whisk in the egg yolk.

With the stand mixer on low speed, slowly add the yeast mixture and blend with the dry ingredients, continuing to mix just until a dough is formed, 2 to 3 minutes.

Spray or brush the inside of a small mixing bowl with vegetable oil. Transfer the dough to the oiled bowl. Cover and allow to sit for 20 minutes at room temperature until the dough increases in size by about half.

Meanwhile, line a baking sheet with parchment paper and brush it with vegetable oil.

Turn the dough out onto a lightly floured surface and divide it into eight portions. Gently form into balls and place on the prepared baking sheet. Cover and refrigerate for at least 2 hours and preferably overnight.

On a lightly floured surface, roll the balls of dough into round or oval flatbreads roughly ¼ inch (6 mm) thick.

Preheat a barbecue to 500°F (260°C).

Place the rolled-out dough directly onto the grill and brush with olive oil. Once the dough starts to bubble, flip it, brush with oil, and season with salt, then cook for 2 to 3 more minutes.

Remove the flatbreads from the grill and allow to rest for 5 minutes before cutting and serving.

¼ cup (60 g) butter
½ cup (125 mL) cream
2 Tbsp (30 mL) milk
5½ cups (690 g) flour
1 Tbsp (10 g) sugar
1¼ tsp (4 g) salt, plus more for seasoning
1½ tsp (7 g) baking powder
1 tsp (3 g) active dry yeast
1 egg yolk
1 cup (250 mL) water (warm if using dry yeast)
Vegetable oil for bowl and baking sheet
Olive oil for grilling

MAKES ABOUT 8 FLATBREADS

Photo on page 69

(Overleaf) Naan-style Bread ▶

Many guests who travel to Tofino are concerned with wellness and health and, not surprisingly, many of them ask for gluten-free options. Executive Chef Barr's team makes this cornbread without wheat flour, and you can easily do the same, substituting regular flour with a gluten-free version like Cup4Cup. It's delicious either way and a perfect accompaniment to a bowl of chowder.

CORNBREAD

2 cups (250 g) all-purpose or
　(275 g) gluten-free flour
¾ cup (125 g) cornmeal
2 Tbsp (30 g) baking powder
1 cup (200 g) sugar
2 tsp (6 g) salt
¾ cup (180 mL) vegetable oil
3 eggs
1 cup (250 mL) buttermilk

**MAKES ONE 8-INCH
(20 CM) SQUARE
CORNBREAD**

Preheat the oven to 325°F (160°C). Spray an 8-inch (20 cm) square baking pan with cooking spray or line with parchment paper.

In a large bowl, sift together the dry ingredients.

In a medium-size bowl, whisk together the oil, eggs, and buttermilk.

Make a well in the dry ingredients and stir in the liquids, mixing until well combined. Pour into the prepared baking pan and place in the oven.

Bake until golden on top and a wooden skewer inserted into the centre comes out clean and dry, 40 to 45 minutes. Bread will keep for a couple of days wrapped in plastic wrap at room temperature.

During Chef Wilson's tenure at the Inn, he became famous for his bread: luscious, chewy, sometimes flavoured, always irresistible. These are delicious on their own warm from the oven, slathered with butter, made into sandwiches, or, best of all, served alongside chowders. This is a basic sourdough loaf made with Tofino Brewing Company's Tuff Session Ale, but any pale ale would work just fine.

Tuff Session SOURDOUGH BREAD

In the bowl of a stand mixer fitted with a dough hook, place the flour, yeast, and sourdough starter and start mixing on slow. Add about three-quarters of the beer and continue mixing for 5 minutes. The dough should be moist but not overly sticky—if it's too dry, add more beer until the desired consistency is reached. After the first 5 minutes, turn the machine up to medium speed and mix for another 5 minutes. Add the salt and continue to mix on medium for a few more minutes.

Remove the dough and knead until its surface is very smooth. Place in a large bowl, cover with plastic wrap, and put aside somewhere warm to allow the dough to come to life. (Technically, this is the autolyse stage, when the flour is absorbing the liquids and its enzymes are breaking down the starches and proteins.) Depending on the temperature of your kitchen, this could take roughly 30 to 45 minutes. Once the dough has expanded slightly and is moist but springy to the touch, divide it into four pieces, then shape each into a ball.

Let the balls of dough rest for 10 minutes covered with a cloth, then place them on a parchment-lined baking sheet and cover with a cloth again. You may need to divide them between two baking sheets. Place them somewhere warm to rise until nearly doubled in size, 3 to 4 hours.

Preheat the oven to 450°F (230°C). Using a serrated knife, slash the tops of the loaves once down the middle, then place the baking sheet in the oven. Using a spray bottle, spritz some water around the inside of the oven to create a bit of steam, then bake the loaves for 15 to 20 minutes or until nicely golden.

8 cups (1 kg) bread flour

1 Tbsp (10 g) active dry yeast

2 cups (500 mL) sourdough starter (see note)

2 to 2⅓ cups (500 to 580 mL) Tofino Brewing Company Tuff Session Ale or other pale ale

2½ Tbsp (25 g) salt

MAKES 4 LOAVES

SOURDOUGH STARTER

You can buy sourdough starter at some gourmet shops and bakeries or order it online. Alternatively, you can make your own: In a non-reactive bowl, mix a package of active dry yeast (2¼ tsp/7 g), 2 cups (250 g) flour, and 2 cups (500 mL) warm water and cover loosely. Leave the starter in a warm place to ferment for about a week. It will be ready when it is bubbly and has a pleasantly tangy aroma. Refrigerate until you're ready to use it. Remember: The starter will last for years as long as you continue to feed it. Store it in a tightly closed container in the refrigerator. Once a week, mix ¼ cup (60 g) sourdough starter together with ¼ cup (60 mL) lukewarm water and just under ½ cup (about 65 g) flour, then stir the mixture back into the starter. And be sure to replenish the starter whenever you use any of it: Replace whatever you've removed from the container with equal amounts of water and flour as well as a pinch of sugar to keep it well fed.

Chef Filatow's hearty, wholesome whole wheat bread is ideal for breakfast, but it also makes a great companion to chowders. Chef Filatow, however, has his own way of enjoying it: straight from the oven. "My favourite thing is to slice a piece off after about 10 minutes and let a piece of sharp cheese melt on it," he says. "Crunchy warm crust with melted cheese!" Note that you will have to start this the day before you bake it.

RUGGED LOAF

1½ Tbsp (10 g) instant dry yeast
4⅔ cups (1.1 L) plus 5 Tbsp
   (75 mL) cold water
2½ cups (200 g) rolled oats
1½ cups (200 g) cracked seven-
   grain cereal
4 cups (500 g) whole wheat flour
4 cups (500 g) bread flour
5 tsp (25 g) sea salt

MAKES 3 LOAVES

In the bowl of a stand mixer, dissolve the yeast in 4⅔ cups (1.1 L) cold water. Add the oats and the cracked grains and mix, using the dough hook. Add the flours and mix until no dry flour remains. Set aside for 30 minutes to rest.

Add the salt and the 5 Tbsp (75 mL) water. Knead the salt into the dough with the water. Knead the dough for 10 minutes by hand or 5 minutes in a stand mixer.

Place the dough in a large bowl and cover with plastic wrap. Refrigerate overnight.

The next day, remove the dough from the fridge and divide into three pieces.

Shape the dough into rustic loaves, place them on a baking sheet, and cover them with a tea towel, then allow to rise in a warm place for 2 to 3 hours.

When you're ready to bake, preheat the oven to 500°F (260°C). Line two baking sheets with parchment paper and arrange the racks in the oven so there is enough room for the bread.

Once the dough has doubled in size, slash the tops with a knife, place them on the prepared baking sheets, and immediately pop them in the oven. Using a spray bottle, mist a little water around the inside of the oven to create a bit of steam.

Bake for 20 minutes, then rotate the baking sheets so the top is on the bottom and the front is to the back. Bake for another 20 minutes or until the tops are golden. Remove the loaves and cool on wire racks.

"Rod hired me over the phone—they were desperate, I guess."

Chef Profile: **MARK FILATOW**

THE WICKANINNISH INN was the springboard for Mark Filatow's current career as chef, sommelier, and partner in Kelowna's Waterfront Wines and Waterfront Café and Catering.

He was part of the team when the Inn opened in August 1996. "Rod [Butters] hired me over the phone—they were desperate, I guess," he jokes. He started as a three-month pastry assistant, then worked as entremetier, responsible for the soups. His most memorable dish? "Well, let's say I made a lot of chowder. A freakin' lot of it!" he says. "But it really taught me a lot about soup and being creative with it."

Reflecting on the two years he worked at The Pointe, he has fond memories of tasting his first Dungeness crab and cycling back to the Inn from the Tofino docks with buckets of live crabs hanging from the handlebars. He recalls cooking with tender scallops, wild "chicken of the woods" mushrooms, and the red huckleberries that grow around the Inn. He remembers carving potlatch bowls with master carver Henry Nolla and DJ–ing "Punk and Funk" night at the Maquinna Hotel in downtown Tofino. Most of all, he remembers proposing to his now wife on Chesterman Beach.

"It is a special place for me," he says. "I was exposed to seasonal ingredients and the best seafood. It set a standard that I hold to today."

◀ *Chef Filatow's Sablefish, Clam, Potato, and Bacon Clam Chowder (recipe on page 63)*

Beach Picnics

▼

SALADS AND GRILLS

> "Three times a week on summer evenings, as the sun sinks toward the horizon, Inn staff light the fires on Chesterman Beach and set the rustic wooden table for a crab cookout."

TUCKED AROUND THE corner of the Inn, far from public eyes, there's a special place called Shell Beach. This secluded stretch of sand and crushed shells is tucked in a hidden bay, protected by forest and rocky outcrops, accessible only by private road, making it an ideal spot for beach picnics and private parties. Some lucky couples have tied the knot here under a shower of rose-petal confetti.

Family salmon barbecues were a regular event on this beach when Charles was a child. It was never a complicated meal: When salmon is as fresh as it is here, all it needs is a bit of salt, pepper, fire, a salad, and maybe something sweet to finish. Sometimes, instead of salmon, it was big, fat beach oysters. Other times, it might have been sweet Dungeness crabs from Clayoquot Sound plunged briefly into roiling seawater—crabmeat is at its best cooked in briny water—requiring nothing but a squeeze of lemon juice and melted butter for dipping.

Today's beach picnics are not much different. Three times a week on summer evenings, as the sun sinks toward the horizon, Inn staff light the fires on Chesterman Beach and set the rustic wooden table for a crab cookout. Guests gather around, settling on seats carved from logs that have washed up on shore. The fragrance of smoke fills the air, along with the sound of happy voices. Alongside the boiled crabs, the salads are fancier than they were back when Charles was a kid, and so are the desserts. But just like then, the fresh air sharpens everyone's appetite, so it's a good thing there's always plenty of food to go around.

Visitors to the Inn in the early days will remember Oyster Jim and his beach oysters: big, briny, and so delicious cooked on the barbecue. Here Chef Labossiere recreates his favourite way to serve beach oysters—rich and decadent with bacon and cream.

"BBQ" BEACH OYSTERS

6 large west coast beach oysters or 12 medium oysters, preferably in the shell, but freshly pre-shucked oysters will also work

¼ lb (110 g) pancetta or double-smoked bacon, diced

1 Tbsp (10 g) flour

1 cup (250 mL) cream

1 tsp (5 mL) hot mustard

Juice of ½ lemon

Fine sea salt to taste

½ cup (55 g) grated aged cheddar or Gruyère cheese

1 bunch green onions, thinly sliced

SERVES 2

If you are using oysters in the shell, preheat a gas grill to 400°F (200°C) or the oven to 375°F (190°C). Place the oysters directly onto the grill or onto a baking sheet and into the oven. Cook until the shells open and you see some liquid coming out of the shells; this should take only a few minutes. Discard any oysters that do not open.

Meanwhile, make the sauce. In a small saucepan, render the pancetta or bacon until crispy. Remove from the pan, dry on paper towel, and reserve 1 Tbsp (15 mL) of the rendered fat.

Whisk the flour into the pan with the fat to form a roux. Whisk in the cream and bring to a gentle simmer; cook for 5 to 10 minutes until it is thick but easily spoonable. Season with the hot mustard, lemon juice, and fine sea salt.

To assemble, remove the tops of the oyster shells and shuck the oysters. If you like, whisk the liquid into the sauce.

You can either return the oysters to their shells, using the shell as a vessel for the oyster and sauce, or place them in small ramekins. In any case, spoon the warm sauce over the oysters, top with pancetta or bacon, cheese, and green onions, and place back on the grill or in the oven.

Bake until bubbly and golden brown, about 10 minutes. Cool for 3 to 5 minutes before serving.

Of British Columbia's five indigenous salmon species, none is more highly prized than the sockeye, with its rosy flesh and robust flavour. The first run of the year, which usually lands in the Inn's kitchen in August, is always cause for celebration. One of Chef Butters's favourite ways to enjoy it is in this sumptuous but simple sandwich. He prefers to use Terra Breads' fig and anise bread; both the homemade mayo and the bread have a delicate licorice flavour that perfectly complements the salty pancetta and rich fish. However, you can use your own favourite artisan bread and store-bought mayo if you prefer.

SOCKEYE SALMON "BLT"

4 thin slices pancetta

2 boneless, skinless fillets sockeye salmon, 3 to 4 oz (85 to 110 g) each

4 slices artisan-style bread

Fennel mayonnaise (page 274)

Leaf lettuce

Tomato slices

SERVES 2

Cook the pancetta slices in a pan or in a 350°F (180°C) oven until crispy. Set aside.

On the grill or on the stovetop over medium-high heat, grill or pan-fry the salmon fillets—this should take only a couple of minutes per side—and keep them warm while you toast the bread.

Generously spread fennel mayonnaise on two slices of the toasted bread. Lay the leaf lettuce, crispy pancetta, and tomato slices on top of the mayo, top with the hot salmon, then finish with the remaining toast slices.

Sockeye Salmon "BLT" with Crab Cappucino (page 66) ▶

TUNA

4 cups (1 L) cold water

7 Tbsp (85 g) cane sugar

7 Tbsp (105 g) fine sea salt

1 lb (450 g) albacore tuna loin

Zest of 1 lemon

1 sprig basil

1¼ cups (310 mL) olive oil

DRESSING

⅜ cup (100 mL) red wine vinegar

Finely grated zest and juice of
   1 lemon, plus more to taste

⅜ cup (50 g) pitted green and
   black olives

¼ cup (60 mL) sundried tomatoes

1 anchovy

1 clove garlic

¼ cup (60 mL) tomato juice

2 Tbsp (10 g) chopped flat-leaf
   parsley

2 Tbsp (15 g) capers, drained

1 cup (250 mL) olive oil, preferably from Kalamata or Sicily

Salt and cracked black pepper

SALAD

Arugula

Cherry tomatoes, halved

Fingerling potatoes, steamed

Green beans, blanched

Roasted red peppers, julienned

Radishes, sliced

Good-quality mixed olives

White anchovies

2 to 4 eggs, hard-boiled and
   halved

Olive oil

Cracked black pepper

SERVES 2 TO 4

From the south of France to Tofino: Chef Labossiere's West Coast take on salade niçoise is bursting with goodness and flavour. Note that he gives no amounts for most of the ingredients, leaving it up to you to decide how much of the eggs, beans, arugula, or other vegetables you want to use. "It is however you like it," he says, "the star being the tuna!" The tuna needs to be refrigerated overnight in brine, so you'll need to start this recipe the day before you want to serve it.

NIÇOISE–STYLE SALAD

PREPARE THE TUNA: In a non-reactive dish, combine the water, sugar, and salt and allow the sugar and salt to dissolve completely. Cut the tuna loin into 1-inch (2.5 cm) thick slices and place in the brine. Cover with plastic wrap and refrigerate for 1 hour. Remove from the brine and towel-dry.

Preheat the oven to 225°F (105°C). In a small ovenproof pan (a loaf pan works well), combine the lemon zest, basil, tuna, and olive oil. Cover the pan with aluminum foil, then place in the oven and confit the tuna for 1 hour or until fully cooked through. Alternatively, use a sous-vide machine and circulate at 135°F (57°C) for 25 minutes. Once the tuna is cooked, allow it to cool completely, leaving it in the oil, then place it in the refrigerator overnight.

MAKE THE DRESSING: In a food processor, place all ingredients except the olive oil and salt and pepper, and blend well. Add the olive oil and process until emulsified. Season to taste with salt, pepper, and, if you like, additional lemon juice.

To assemble the salad: Remove the tuna from the oil and towel-dry. Break into large chunks.

In a large bowl, combine all the vegetables—arugula, tomatoes, potatoes, green beans, roasted red peppers, radishes, and olives—and toss with the dressing.

Divide the salad between plates or bowls. Garnish each with a white anchovy, hard-boiled egg, and chunks of tuna. Finish with a drizzle of olive oil and cracked black pepper.

The original Waldorf salad was an unlikely combination of apples, celery, and mayonnaise created in 1896 at the famous New York hotel. It became a hit, especially once grapes and walnuts were added to the mix. Here Executive Chef Barr brings it to the west coast with the addition of smoked salmon and an irresistible walnut dressing made with verjus, an acidic freshly pressed grape juice.

West Coast WALDORF SALAD

MAKE THE DRESSING: In a blender, place all the ingredients except the salt and pepper and process, adding more verjus as needed, until thick and creamy. Season with salt and pepper.

MAKE THE SALAD: Chiffonade the romaine lettuce and kale, then toss the greens with a bit of the dressing. Divide the greens between four bowls, forming them into a nest. Dice the apples and place on top of each nest along with the toasted walnuts, grapes, and sliced celery. Break the hot-smoked salmon into small pieces and divide among the salads. Top each salad with crumbled blue cheese.

Drizzle the remaining dressing over each salad and squeeze a little mayonnaise on top. Finish with a touch of salt and some cracked black pepper.

WALNUT AND VERJUS DRESSING

¾ cup (100 g) walnut halves
½ cup (125 mL) canola oil
¼ cup (60 mL) walnut oil
½ cup (125 mL) verjus, plus additional as needed
2 Tbsp (30 mL) champagne vinegar
2 Tbsp (30 mL) honey
Salt and cracked black pepper to taste

SALAD

1 head romaine lettuce, outer leaves removed
1 bunch kale, leaves only
2 Granny Smith apples
½ cup (70 g) toasted walnut halves
30 red grapes, halved
½ stalk celery, sliced diagonally
¼ lb (110 g) hot-smoked salmon
3 oz (90 g) blue cheese
¼ cup (60 mL) mayonnaise, in a squeeze bottle
Salt and cracked black pepper to taste

SERVES 4

Salads don't always get the respect they deserve, but Chef Ly's bright, aromatic vinaigrette makes this one irresistible. The beets and fennel can be roasted ahead of time, making for quick assembly of the salad at the last minute. It's easy to bump up the quantities, too, for a dinner party or family dinner.

ROASTED BEET and FENNEL SALAD with CITRUS-MINT VINAIGRETTE

SALAD

8 small beets

3 Tbsp (45 mL) olive oil

Salt and cracked black pepper to taste

2 small bulbs fennel

2 sprigs flat-leaf parsley, leaves only

1 handful baby arugula

Pecorino romano cheese to taste

CITRUS-MINT VINAIGRETTE

Juice of 1 orange

Juice of 1 lemon

Juice of 1 lime

⅜ cup (100 mL) olive oil

1 Tbsp (15 mL) honey

Pinch of salt

2 to 4 sprigs mint, leaves only

SERVES 2

Preheat the oven to 350°F (180°C). Toss the beets in half of the olive oil and season to taste with salt and pepper. Place in a baking pan and roast in the oven until fork-tender, 60 to 90 minutes.

Meanwhile, cut the fennel into quarters, toss in the remaining olive oil, and season to taste with salt and pepper. Roast in the oven at the same temperature for about 20 minutes.

Remove the vegetables from the oven and cool to room temperature; this can be done a day ahead of time.

MAKE THE VINAIGRETTE: In a blender, place the citrus juices, olive oil, honey, salt, and mint leaves and purée.

Peel the beets, then toss them with the fennel and parsley in some of the citrus-mint vinaigrette and divide between two plates. Toss the arugula with some of the dressing, season with salt and pepper, and arrange on top of the beets. Grate a bit of pecorino romano cheese overtop, and serve.

Such a simple salad, but with so much depth. Chef Filatow roasts asparagus spears, then tosses them with a savoury dressing made with miso, a Japanese paste of fermented soy beans. (It's a dressing you'll want to make again and again.) Alpine Gold cheese from Farm House Natural Cheeses in Agassiz, BC, adds an irresistible finish.

ROASTED ASPARAGUS SALAD with
Farm House Alpine Gold CHEESE and MISO DRESSING

MISO DRESSING

1 Tbsp (17 g) red miso

3 Tbsp (45 mL) vegetable oil

2 Tbsp (30 mL) apple cider
  vinegar

SALAD

2 Tbsp (18 g) unsalted sunflower
  seeds

24 spears asparagus, tough
  bottoms of spears removed

1 Tbsp (15 mL) olive oil

Sea salt to taste

3 oz (85 g) Farm House Alpine
  Gold or other semi-soft cow's
  milk cheese, thinly sliced

Sunflower shoots (optional)

Thinly sliced red onions or
  shallots (optional)

SERVES 4

MAKE THE DRESSING: In a large non-reactive bowl, whisk the miso, oil, and vinegar together, then set aside.

MAKE THE SALAD: In a small frying pan, lightly toast the sunflower seeds. Set aside to cool.

Toss the asparagus in the olive oil and season with salt.

Heat a cast-iron pan over high heat, then add the asparagus and cook just until lightly charred but still fairly firm. (Alternatively, you could grill the asparagus on a hot barbecue.)

Immediately toss the asparagus in the miso dressing, then divide evenly between four small plates. Place the cheese slices on the asparagus, then sprinkle with the toasted sunflower seeds. Drizzle with any remaining miso dressing. If you like, garnish with some sunflower shoots and thinly sliced red onions or shallots.

Executive Chef Barr's carrot salad is much more than a simple side dish made with a humble vegetable. It is a symphony of flavours, colours, and textures, from a crunchy granola to a silky purée, an aromatic curry, and the crisp sweetness of heirloom carrots. This is a dish designed to impress—and to enjoy.

Curried CARROT SALAD

CURRY GRANOLA

⅓ cup (70 g) dried lentils
1 cup (250 mL) water
1½ cups (120 g) rolled oats
¾ cup (185 mL) canola oil, plus additional to toast the oats
1 cup (80 g) puffed wild rice (see below)
1 cup (120 g) chopped pistachios
1 cup (29 g) crispy rice cereal
3 Tbsp (18 g) curry powder
2 tsp (6 g) salt
1 cup (250 mL) honey

LIME YOGURT

1 cup (250 mL) plain, whole yogurt
Finely grated zest and juice of 2 limes
2 Tbsp (30 mL) honey

CARROT PURÉE

2 large carrots
Salt
Juice of 1 lime
1 Tbsp (15 mL) honey

CURRY VINAIGRETTE

Juice of 3 limes
1 shallot, sliced
1 Tbsp honey
1 cup (250 mL) curry oil (page 260)
Salt and cracked black pepper to taste

Photo on page 96

MAKE THE CURRY GRANOLA: Preheat the oven to 275°F (135°C) and line a large baking sheet with parchment paper.

In a small pot, place the lentils and water and bring to a boil. Cover, reduce heat to a bare simmer, and cook just until tender, about 15 minutes. Drain and cool.

Toss the oats with a bit of canola oil, place in a baking dish, and lightly toast in the oven. Cool slightly.

In a large bowl, mix together all the dry ingredients and seasonings. In a small pot, combine the ¾ cup (180 mL) canola oil and the honey and bring to a boil. Pour over the dry ingredients and mix well.

Scrape the granola mix onto the prepared baking sheet and place in the oven. Bake for 20 minutes or until crunchy and dry. Stir as needed, but be careful not to overmix while it bakes to avoid breaking up the clumps. Remove from the oven and cool.

MAKE THE LIME YOGURT: In a small bowl, combine the yogurt, lime zest and juice, and honey. Mix well.

MAKE THE CARROT PURÉE: Peel and slice the carrots very thinly. In a wide pot, combine the carrots with some salt and just enough water to cover them. Cover with a sheet of parchment paper and boil until the water has evaporated. The carrot slices should be very soft; if not, add more water and continue to cook. In a blender or food processor, purée the carrots until smooth. Season with salt, lime juice, and honey.

MAKE THE CURRY VINAIGRETTE: In a blender, combine the lime juice, shallots, and honey. With the blender running, drizzle in the curry oil. Adjust seasoning as needed.

PREPARE THE CARROTS: Using a mandoline, slice two carrots of different colour into thin coins. Reserve in ice water for later use.

Set a steamer over boiling water. Peel the remaining carrots, place them in the steamer, and steam them lightly. They should not be raw, but should still have a fair bit of crunch to them. Place them in a large bowl, drizzle with lime juice and curry oil, sprinkle with salt, and mix well.

ASSEMBLE THE SALADS: In the centre of six plates, place dollops of lime yogurt and carrot purée, creating a circle around the centre of the plate.

Cut the cooked carrots into lengths of about ½ to 1 inch (2.5 cm to 3 cm) and dress in the curry vinaigrette. Arrange the raw sliced carrots and the cooked carrots all standing up in the yogurt/purée circles on the plates. Drizzle dill oil onto and around the carrots. Finish the dish with some curry granola for texture and some dill fronds.

CARROT SALAD

4 bunches medium-size rainbow
   carrots
Juice of 2 limes
⅓ cup (80 mL) curry oil
   (page 260)
Salt to taste
Dill oil (page 260)
2 sprigs dill fronds

SERVES 6

Puffed Wild Rice

In a small sauce pot, heat the oil until it reaches 450°F (230°). Drop in the wild rice and cook until well puffed; this should just take a few seconds. Remove the puffed rice with a slotted spoon and drain on paper towels. Season with salt.

2 cups (500 mL) canola oil
⅓ cup (50 g) wild rice
Salt to taste

MAKES ABOUT 1 CUP (80 G)

Chef Springett's dense and savoury pork pie makes a satisfying lunch to tuck into a picnic basket and enjoy on a windswept beach. It requires the use of a traditional hot-water crust, made richer here with the addition of an egg and butter. At once humble and sophisticated, this is a great addition to any cook's repertoire.

TRADITIONAL PORK PIE with WINE JELLY

FILLING

10 oz (300 g) pork belly, skin removed, diced small

10 oz (300 g) pork shoulder, diced small

2 anchovies in oil, drained and finely chopped

2 Tbsp (4 g) sage, finely sliced

Pinch of freshly grated nutmeg

Salt and cracked black pepper to taste

7 oz (200 g) bacon or pancetta, cut into matchstick-size slices

HOT-WATER DOUGH

3 cups (375 g) flour

1 egg

¾ cup (170 g) butter

¾ cup (185 mL) water

1 tsp (3 g) salt

1 tsp (4 g) sugar

EGG WASH

1 egg

1 tsp (5 mL) cream

WINE JELLY

2 Tbsp (30 mL) water

2 tsp (8 g) powdered gelatin

¾ cup + 2 Tbsp (215 mL) pork or chicken stock

6 Tbsp (90 mL) port or sherry

MAKES 8 INDIVIDUAL PIES

MAKE THE FILLING: Chill all the ingredients to 39°F (4°C) before processing. (Note: This is the interior temperature of most refrigerators, so just be sure to chill everything for a few hours or overnight.)

On a large cutting board, finely chop the chilled pork belly, pork shoulder, and anchovies. Place into a bowl and mix in the spices. Refrigerate for 15 minutes, then fold in the bacon or pancetta.

In a sauté pan, cook a tablespoon off to check the seasoning. Adjust the salt and pepper if needed. Return to the refrigerator.

MAKE THE HOT-WATER DOUGH: Place the flour in a large bowl and make a well in the centre. In a separate small bowl, lightly whisk the egg.

In a small pot set over medium-high heat, place the butter, water, salt, and sugar and bring to a boil, stirring constantly. Count to 30, then pour about half this liquid into the well in the flour, stirring with a wooden spoon while adding the hot liquid.

Add a bit of the hot liquid to the egg, whisking it quickly, then pour the egg mixture into the flour, stirring it constantly. (This should temper the egg so it doesn't cook.)

Stir in the remaining hot liquid to form a sticky dough. Cover with a towel and let it rest for 1 hour.

Preheat the oven to 375°F (190°C).

Lightly grease and flour eight small pie moulds, medium-size ramekins, or large muffin tins. Tap out any excess flour and arrange the moulds on a rimmed baking sheet.

Turn the dough out onto a floured surface and, using your hands, press it into a rectangle. Fold the dough like a book and press again into a rectangle.

Roll the dough into a ¼-inch (6 mm) thick rectangle, fold like a book again, and roll out to ⅛ inch (3 mm) thick. Cover and let the dough rest for 10 minutes.

Recipe continues ▶

Cut eight large round bases and eight small round tops out of the dough—the bottoms should be large enough to fill the bottom and sides of your pie dishes (moulds, ramekins, or muffin tins) with a little extra overhang, and the tops should fit like a lid. (Create a stencil using parchment paper to make sure the dough fits properly.)

Line the greased and floured pie dishes with the pastry base, making sure the pastry sits slightly above the edge of the dishes and is pressed snugly against the sides and bottom. Make sure there are no cracks in the pastry.

Divide the filling mixture evenly between the pie dishes, making sure to fill every nook and cranny.

Whisk together the eggs and cream to form an egg wash, then paint it over the edges of the top of the pastry. Cover with the small pastry rounds. Pinch the edges closed, making sure you have a good seal. Brush lightly with egg wash and poke a vent hole in the top of each.

Bake the pies until they reach an internal temperature of 160°F (71°C), 45 minutes to 1 hour. (Use an instant-read thermometer to be sure they are fully cooked.) Remove from the oven and cool to room temperature.

MAKE THE WINE JELLY: In a bowl, stir the water and powdered gelatin together to dissolve the gelatin, and let sit for 10 minutes. In a small pot, bring the stock and port to a simmer. Add the gelatin water to the pot and cook for a couple of minutes, making sure it is completely dissolved. Remove from the heat and cool.

Using a squeeze bottle, squeeze the jelly through the vent holes into the pies, then place in the refrigerator to set overnight. Serve the pies with a grainy mustard or red onion marmalade and a light salad.

KALE TAPENADE

Traditional tapenade is made with briny olives for an earthy, salty flavour. Here Executive Chef Barr uses kale for the earthiness and adds those briny notes with capers and anchovies to create a dip that goes nicely with Mediterranean dishes or hearty crudités. The anchovies can be omitted to make the tapenade vegan. This also makes a great sandwich spread.

In a blender or food processor, combine the capers, garlic, anchovies, olive oil, lemon zest and juice, and pumpkin seeds and purée until smooth. Add the kale and continue processing until smooth. Season to taste with salt and pepper.

⅓ cup (45 g) capers, brine
    squeezed out
1 to 2 cloves garlic
1 to 2 anchovies
¼ cup (60 mL) oil (extra-virgin
    olive oil, canola, or sunflower)
Finely grated zest and juice of
    1 lemon
¼ cup (35 g) raw pumpkin seeds
2 cups (135 g) chopped kale,
    leaves only
Salt and cracked black pepper

**MAKES ABOUT 1½ CUPS
(375 ML)**

SUNFLOWER SEED CHEESE

Executive Chef Barr's seedy spread makes a wonderfully cheesy appetizer for your vegan friends, but is delicious enough for carnivores to enjoy. Spread it on crackers or grilled bread, or serve with raw vegetables.

In a small pot, place the sunflower seeds, baking soda, and a pinch of salt and add enough water to cover. Simmer for 25 minutes, then add the garlic and simmer for another 5 minutes. Drain and rinse under fresh water.

    Place the seeds in the bowl of a food processor along with the nutritional yeast, canola oil, mustard, lemon juice, and ½ cup (125 mL) water. Blend until smooth, adding more water if necessary. Season with salt.

2 cups (285 g) unsalted sunflower
    seeds
½ tsp (2 g) baking soda
Salt to taste
6 cloves garlic
½ cup (30 g) nutritional yeast
¼ cup (60 mL) cold-pressed
    canola oil
3 Tbsp (15 mL) Dijon mustard
Juice of 2 lemons

**MAKES ABOUT 2 CUPS
(500 ML)**

"The Inn taught me that a chef is more than somebody who runs a kitchen, and a restaurant can be more than just a place that serves food."

Chef Profile: WARREN BARR

GROWING UP IN Vancouver, Warren Barr had long heard about the Wickaninnish Inn, but he had never ventured as far west as Tofino. Instead, after starting out as an apprentice at Vancouver's legendary Le Crocodile, his career took him east to Prince Edward Island, where he became chef at the farm-to-table Inn at Bay Fortune. In winters, when the inn was closed, he'd work in some of Montreal's top restaurants. After six years, he wanted to be closer to his parents, who had just retired, and his brother, who had young children. He called a friend who was working at the Wickaninnish Inn, and joined the team in 2011. Two years later, in April 2013, he became executive chef.

East, west, or somewhere in between, defining Canadian cuisine has always been a mission of Chef Barr's. He has a passion for local, seasonal, and responsibly grown ingredients, and he works closely with local pros like fisherman Jeff Mikus, forager Alexander McNaughton, and members of the Tofino Ucluelet Culinary Guild to source the very best BC products. Then he transforms them into ambitious dishes that take Canadian cuisine to a whole new level. "The Inn has encouraged me to follow that path while exposing me to more discerning and worldly guests," he says. "I have been able to pursue Canadian cuisine in a very refined manner, which has been a unique and special experience."

That could mean discovering the flavour potential of local ingredients like hemlock tips—spruce and fir may be trendy, he says, but hemlock has a delicate, citrusy flavour that is a natural pairing for the wonderful local seafood. It could mean taking a childhood favourite and transforming it into a decadently flavourful vegetarian dish, as he does with his carrot bolognaise. It could mean heading out on the road with his sous chefs and learning from collaborations with other chefs.

Most importantly, he says, "the Wickaninnish Inn has taught me that a chef is more than somebody who runs a kitchen, and a restaurant can be more than just a place that serves food. Here we strive to create an experience and deliver something personal to our guests that they will hold on to for the rest of their lives."

◀ *Executive Chef Barr's Curried Carrot Salad (recipe on page 90)*

By the Fire

▼

CASUAL FARE

No need to dress up. No need even for cutlery. Life can really be this easy.

DARKNESS FALLS, SLOWLY, then suddenly. This far from town, when darkness comes, it is absolute. The only bright spots are the mellow lights flickering from homes tucked into the woods along Chesterman Beach and, on a clear night, the icy twinkle of millions of stars overhead. Off in the distance, there might be a flash from a lighthouse, sometimes a gleam of light from a passing ship. Otherwise the night is inky, a little daunting, the dark forest breathless with the unknown.

But here by the fire, things are warm and bright and tasty.

Guests relax on the cozy sofas by the Driftwood Café's stone fireplace, with its sea-worn wood mantel, sipping wine and snacking on cheese and charcuterie. Over in The Pointe, a copper fireplace is the central focus of the room, just like the old wood-burning stove that warmed Charles's home when he was growing up. On one side of the flames, guests dine on fine cuisine; on the other, tucked away in the bar, they enjoy chowder and burgers.

And sometimes, staying in is the most relaxing way to spend an evening, lounging in front of your own guest-room fireplace, indulging in room service and never having to leave the flames.

Although the Inn is known for exceptionally fine cuisine, our casual fare can be just as satisfying. No need to dress up. No need even for cutlery. Life can really be this easy; food, this friendly and delicious.

Order a glass of wine or a local beer and watch the flames dance merrily. The night may be dark, the skies threatening with rain, but here by the fire, life is good.

Executive Chef Barr's crispy vegetarian snack makes a hearty treat to enjoy on a chilly, rainy day as you curl up in front of the fire. Delicious on their own, the fried polenta cubes are even better with a spicy dip made with sambal oelek, the zingy Southeast Asian chili sauce.

FRIED POLENTA with SPICY AIOLI

MAKE THE POLENTA: Line an 8- × 12-inch (20 × 30 cm) baking pan with non-stick foil, making sure there is substantial overhang to help lift the polenta out. Set aside.

In a medium-size pot, combine the milk and vegetable stock and bring to a boil. Whisk in 2 cups (300 g) cornmeal and simmer for 15 minutes, stirring frequently. Transfer to a double boiler and simmer under plastic wrap for 30 minutes. It should be very thick.

Remove from the heat and stir in the cream cheese, mashed garlic, butter, and oil. Season with espelette, salt, and black pepper. Spread in the prepared pan 1 inch (2.5 cm) thick. Cool in the fridge until firmly set, about four hours.

Line a large baking sheet with parchment paper. When the polenta has cooled and set firmly, cut it into 1-inch (2.5 cm) cubes, spray lightly with water, then toss in 1½ cups (225 g) fine cornmeal. Arrange on the baking sheet so there is some space between the cubes, and leave uncovered in the fridge overnight to form a skin.

MAKE THE SPICY AIOLI: In a small bowl, mix the mayonnaise and sambal oelek together. Cover and refrigerate until needed.

FINISH THE POLENTA: When you're ready to fry the polenta, preheat the oven to 200°F (95°C) and place a baking sheet lined with parchment paper in the oven.

In a deep pan, heat about 4 cups (1 L) cooking oil to 350°F (180°C). Use a thermometer to ensure the temperature is accurate. Working quickly and carefully, fry the polenta cubes in batches. They are done when they are crisp and golden, 3 to 5 minutes. Using a skimmer, scoop the cubes out and place them on the paper-towel-lined baking sheet in the oven to drain some of the oil and to keep the polenta warm while you finish the remaining batches. Serve the polenta cubes warm with the spicy aioli.

POLENTA
4 cups (1 L) milk
4 cups (1 L) vegetable stock
3½ cups (525 g) fine cornmeal
⅔ cup (150 g) cream cheese
10 cloves roasted garlic, mashed (see page 130)
¼ cup (60 g) butter
⅓ cup (80 mL) garlic oil or vegetable oil
Espelette pepper to taste
Salt to taste
Cracked black pepper to taste
Canola or vegetable oil for frying

SPICY AIOLI
1 cup (250 mL) mayonnaise
¼ cup (60 mL) sambal oelek

SERVES A CROWD

Photo on page 107

Puffy, crisp, and mildly flavoured, Executive Chef Barr's buttermilk crackers are an elegant accompaniment to soft cheeses, dips, gravlax, and tuna tartare, or even alongside a rich seafood chowder. Make the crackers in different shapes and sizes and arrange them in a basket for a dramatic presentation.

BUTTERMILK CRACKERS

5 cups (625 g) flour, plus additional for kneading and rolling the dough

1 Tbsp (10 g) sugar

1 tsp (3 g) salt

1 cup (230 g) cold butter

2 egg whites

1 cup (250 mL) buttermilk

Coarse sea salt for sprinkling

SERVES A CROWD

Sift the flour and place in the bowl of a stand mixer, then add the sugar and salt. Cut the cold butter into 1-inch (2.5 cm) cubes and toss through the flour mix. Using the paddle attachment, cut the butter into the flour on the lowest speed until the mixture has a crumb-like consistency.

In a separate bowl, whisk the egg whites together with the buttermilk. With the mixer running, pour the liquid ingredients into the dry ones. Continue to mix until the dough comes together; it may be crumbly.

Remove the dough from the bowl and place it on a lightly floured surface. Knead for a few minutes to bring it all together. Form the dough into a ball, cover in plastic wrap, and let it rest in the refrigerator for at least 1 hour or, for best results, overnight.

When you're ready to bake the crackers, preheat the oven to 350°F (180°C) and line two baking sheets with parchment paper.

On a floured surface, roll the dough out to about ½ inch (1 cm) thick and cut into manageable squares 2 to 3 inches (5 to 8 cm) wide. Set a pasta machine to the widest setting, then run the first piece of dough through it, repeating on ever narrower settings until you go as thin as you can without tearing the dough. Flour generously between each setting to ensure your dough doesn't stick and tear.

Repeat with the remaining dough. Cut into whatever size pieces you like—really big ones look impressive, but smaller ones are more manageable—and arrange on the prepared baking sheets. (You'll likely have to bake these in several batches.)

Mist the crackers with water, then sprinkle with coarse salt. Bake for about 10 minutes, rotating baking sheets after about 5 minutes, or until the crackers are golden and puffed.

Sweetness and smoke combine to transform salmon into an irresistible snack. Chef Labossiere's take on the west coast favourite makes a great appetizer or part of a charcuterie board. Note that this will take several days to make, including time to brine and rest before smoking.

CANDIED SALMON

DAY 1: In a heatproof, non-reactive container big enough to hold about a gallon (4 L), combine all the brine ingredients and mix well. Allow the brine to cool to room temperature, stirring occasionally to ensure the sugar and salt are dissolved. Cover and refrigerate until very cold, ideally overnight.

DAY 2: Cut the salmon into approximately 1- × 4-inch (2.5 × 10 cm) strips, leaving the skin on. Place the salmon strips into a large plastic container and cover with the brine. Gently stir the salmon with a wooden spoon or silicone spatula. Brine for 18 hours in the refrigerator, stirring the fish every 6 hours or so.

DAY 3: Remove the fish from the brine and place on baking sheets lined with drying racks. Refrigerate, uncovered, for 24 to 48 hours or until the salmon is completely dry to the touch.

DAY 4: Preheat a smoker to 145°F (63°C), and smoke the fish over half alder and half apple chips for about 2 hours or until completely cooked. For the last half hour or so, open the smoker vents to allow all the moisture to escape.

Leave the salmon to rest at room temperature for 2 to 3 hours. Coat the smoked salmon in maple syrup and store in a sealed container or in vacuum packs. Freeze or refrigerate until ready to enjoy.

BRINE

1 cup (240 g) fine sea salt
1 cup (250 mL) tamari
¾ cup (185 mL) good-quality
   honey
1 cup (220 g) packed brown sugar
¾ cup (185 mL) maple syrup
10 cups (2.5 L) hot (not boiling)
   water

SALMON

5 lb (2.2 kg) boneless, skin-on
   salmon fillets
1 cup (250 mL) maple syrup

MAKES ABOUT 4 LB (1.8 KG)

Crispy and toothsome, Executive Chef Barr's hearty fish fritters make a satisfying snack alongside a glass of beer or a cocktail at On the Rocks Lounge.

FISH FRITTERS

¼ cup (60 mL) canola oil, plus
    additional for frying
1 cup (165 g) corn kernels
4 cloves garlic, finely chopped
2 cups (228 g) masa harina
1 red bell pepper, seeded and
    diced
½ red onion, diced small
3 sprigs dill, chopped
9 oz (270 g) hot-smoked fish,
    skin and bones removed, diced
Finely grated zest and juice of
    2 lemons
¼ to ½ cup (60 to 125 mL) water
Salt to taste
Hot sauce and mayonnaise, to
    serve

SERVES 4

In a wide pan, heat the ¼ cup (60 mL) canola oil over medium heat, add the corn kernels, and roast for a few minutes. When the kernels begin to brown, add the finely chopped garlic and cook for a further 30 seconds. Remove from the heat and cool for a couple of minutes.

In a large bowl, combine the masa harina with the red peppers, onions, and dill. Gently stir in the fish, then the lemon zest and juice. Drizzle ¼ cup (60 mL) hot water into the mixture until it becomes a thick paste that you can work with your hands; add more water if necessary to achieve the right consistency.

Heat the oven to 350°F (180°C). Fill a deep pot about halfway full with the canola oil and heat it to 350°F (180°C)—use a frying thermometer for greater accuracy. Use your hands to shape the fish fritters into rough shapes with lots of ridges. Fry the fritters until golden brown, then drain on paper towels. Transfer to a baking sheet, season with salt, and place in the oven for a few minutes or until the fritters are hot in the centre. Serve with hot sauce and mayonnaise.

Fish Fritters and Fried Polenta (recipe on page 103) served with hot sauce ▶

Picture British Columbia's west coast and thoughts of salmon won't be far behind. Executive Chef Barr's recipe for a simple but flavourful gravlax makes the most of the bountiful and sustainable wild fish. Perfect for canapés or as part of a seafood charcuterie platter, this is one party dish you will make again and again.

Wickaninnish Inn SALMON GRAVLAX

1 cup (145 g) salt

1 cup (200 g) sugar

Finely grated zest of 1 orange

Finely grated zest of ½ grapefruit

Finely grated zest of 1 lemon

Finely grated zest of 1 lime

1 Tbsp (5 g) toasted fennel seeds, crushed

2 sprigs dill, leaves only, chopped

1 side fresh coho or sockeye salmon

SERVES 8 TO 10

In a small non-reactive bowl, combine all the ingredients, except the salmon, and mix well. This is the cure.

Remove the pin bones from the salmon. Rub the cure onto both sides of the salmon, making sure the flesh is completely covered. (You may not use all of the cure mixture.) Wrap the salmon tightly in plastic wrap and store on a tray in the fridge for 6 to 8 hours.

Rinse off the cure, then put the salmon back on the tray and leave it uncovered in the fridge to air-dry overnight.

Slice the salmon thinly, being sure to leave the skin behind. Serve with crackers, bread, cream cheese, capers, red onions, and pickles.

Salmon gets all the attention on the west coast, but these waters are also home to the albacore tuna, a sustainable fish with a rich pale flesh ideal for enjoying raw or lightly cured. In this recipe, Executive Chef Barr adds the delicate flavours of herbs and citrus to create an irresistible appetizer or light meal.

ALBACORE TUNA TARTARE

¼ cup (60 mL) canola oil, plus
    additional as needed
3 Tbsp (45 mL) apple cider
    vinegar
1 shallot, finely chopped
Finely grated zest of ½ lemon
1 small Granny Smith apple, diced
    small
1 lb (450 g) albacore tuna loin,
    trimmed of any ragged bits
Salt to taste
3 sprigs dill, leaves only
1 sprig mint, leaves only, chopped
3 sprigs flat-leaf parsley, leaves
    only, chopped

SERVES 6

Make the marinade by mixing together the canola oil, vinegar, shallots, and lemon zest. Stir in the diced apple.

Dice the tuna, mix with the marinade, and season with salt. Divide the tartare between six plates; if you have one, use a ring mould to shape the tuna into a compact disc.

Toss the herbs with just enough canola oil to coat them, then arrange them on top of the tuna tartare. Serve with buttermilk crackers (page 104).

INN-STYLE

This is a beautiful and satisfying dish as is, but it can be extraordinary if you make it Inn-style the way Executive Chef Barr does. Using a small round mould, he creates a compact tower of the tartare. In a small bowl, he then combines ½ cup (125 mL) leek oil (page 259) with 1 cup (250 mL) buttermilk and spoons it around the tartare. It creates an elegant marbling effect and an additional layer of flavour.

In Clayoquot Sound, Dungeness crab is in season year-round. Tofitians enjoy this tender local crustacean in a myriad of ways—simmered in chowders, boiled and dipped in butter, grilled over an open flame—but Chef Butters makes the most of it with a simple crab cake that emphasizes the sweet flavours of the crabmeat. At once elegant and casual, this makes a terrific starter course or party nibble. He suggests pairing this with the classic Mission Hill Family Estate 2014 Reserve Chardonnay.

CRAB CAKES

Purée the fish in a food processor until smooth. Refrigerate until ready to use.

In a small pan on medium heat, heat the grapeseed oil. When it is hot, add the onions, celery, and fennel and cook until the vegetables are soft and translucent. Do not brown. Remove from the heat and chill.

In a bowl, combine the puréed fish, chilled vegetables, herbs, egg, cream, and crabmeat. Form into four equal-size cakes and refrigerate until ready to use.

Meanwhile, prepare the salsa verde and celeriac slaw (recipes follow).

When you're ready to cook the crab cakes: Preheat a non-stick pan over medium heat. Add a small amount of oil and butter.

Place the crab cakes into the pan and cook on one side until golden brown. Flip over and continue cooking until done. This should take 8 to 14 minutes in total, depending on the thickness. Poke a wooden skewer or knife into the centre of one of the cakes to check if it is cooked through.

Spoon the salsa verde onto four small plates and place a crab cake on each plate. Garnish with celeriac slaw and serve.

6 oz (170 g) white fish, such as snapper or cod, deboned
1 Tbsp (15 mL) grapeseed oil
¼ cup (30 g) finely chopped onion
¼ cup (25 g) very small–diced celery
¼ cup (20 g) very small–diced fennel
1 Tbsp (5 g) chopped chervil or tarragon
1 egg
¼ cup (60 mL) whipping cream
½ lb (225 g) crabmeat
Salsa verde (recipe overleaf)
Celeriac slaw (recipe overleaf)
Oil and butter, as needed

SERVES 4

Salsa Verde

2 large dill pickles

2 anchovies

3 cloves garlic

1 tsp (5 mL) sambal oelek

1 Tbsp (15 mL) lemon juice

1½ Tbsp (15 g) capers

¼ cup (15 g) chopped flat-leaf
parsley leaves

⅛ cup (5 g) chopped mint leaves

¼ cup (60 mL) olive oil

**MAKES ABOUT 1 CUP
(250 ML)**

Put all ingredients in a food processor and purée, but leave somewhat chunky. Transfer to a sealed container and refrigerate until ready to use. Can be made a day ahead.

Celeriac Slaw

¾ cup (75 g) julienned or
shredded celeriac

½ Tbsp (3 g) mustard seeds

3 Tbsp (45 mL) mayonnaise

**MAKES ABOUT ¾ CUP
(185 ML)**

Toss together the ingredients and refrigerate until ready to serve.

It's not just the sea that's bountiful around Vancouver Island. So are its inland lakes, where rainbow and cutthroat trout abound. Local outfitters can arrange fishing trips, but there's no need to catch your own when you can enjoy Executive Chef Barr's cured trout lightly glazed with a fragrant blend of fruit and floral notes.

ELDERFLOWER– and GRAPE–GLAZED TROUT

CURE THE TROUT: In a small non-reactive bowl, combine the salt, sugar, zest, and grated beet and mix well. Remove the skin and pin bones from the trout and place on a small tray. Cover with the cure mixture and place in the refrigerator for 1 hour, then wash off and pat the trout dry. Transfer the trout to a clean tray and return to the fridge.

Meanwhile, make the glaze: In a small pot, bring the grape juice, sugar, vinegar, and vermouth to a boil and cook for 5 minutes. Add the pectin and boil for 5 more minutes, then add lemon juice and remove from the heat. Place in a bowl, cover, and cool in the fridge. Once cooled, brush the glaze onto the trout, repeating every hour for 3 hours.

TO FINISH: Preheat the oven to 200°F (95°C) and line a baking sheet with parchment paper. Once the oven has reached temperature, turn it off. Place the trout on a baking sheet and into the oven to cook gently. The fillets are ready when they start to pull apart where pressure is applied. This may take 5 to 15 minutes.

Serve with crackers (such as the buttermilk crackers on page 104) or bread and cream cheese.

TROUT

½ cup (75 g) salt
½ cup (100 g) sugar
Finely grated zest of ½ orange
Finely grated zest of 1 lemon
1 small red beet, peeled and grated
2 sides trout

GLAZE

⅞ cup (200 mL) pulp-free Coronation or Concord grape juice
¼ cup (50 g) sugar
¼ cup (60 mL) elderflower vinegar (page 258)
2 Tbsp (30 mL) dry vermouth
1 package liquid pectin, such as Certo
Juice of ½ lemon

SERVES 4 TO 6

Chorizo adds a zingy Spanish flavour to Chef Butters's simple steamed shellfish dish—the early explorers of these waters, such as Spain's Captain Juan Pérez, would have been pleased. This makes an easy lunch with crusty bread and a craft beer, or a satisfying first course at dinner. He suggests pairing it with a bold ale such as BNA Brewing Co.'s Don't Lose Your Dinosaur IPA from Kelowna.

MUSSELS and CLAMS

2 Tbsp (30 mL) olive oil

2 shallots, diced

2 to 4 cloves garlic

1 dried chorizo sausage, diced small

1 lb (450 g) mussels, rinsed well in cold water, any opened shells discarded

1 lb (450 g) clams, rinsed well in cold water, any opened shells discarded

⅓ cup (80 mL) chicken stock

1 medium tomato, diced

5 basil leaves, torn

1 Tbsp (5 g) chopped flat-leaf parsley

¼ cup (40 g) peas, fresh or frozen and thawed

SERVES 2 TO 4

Heat a large pot over medium-high heat. Add the oil, and when it's hot, add the shallots, garlic, and chorizo. Stir and cook quickly until the sausage is a little crispy.

Add the mussels and clams. Stir with the sausage mixture. Cook for 1 minute. Add the chicken stock and cover the pot with a lid. Cook until the shells open fully, approximately 4 to 6 minutes. Discard any mussels or clams that do not open.

Gently stir in the tomatoes, basil, parsley, and peas. Divide between two or four bowls (depending on whether you're serving this as an appetizer or a main course) and serve with a warm baguette for dipping into the broth.

The mussels that grow in the waters off Vancouver Island are sweet and plump, a perfect match for Chef Labossiere's fragrant Thai green curry sauce. The sauce itself could easily be made a day ahead of time, making it a snap to pull this dish together for a quick supper or lunch. Just be sure to offer plenty of bread to soak up every delicious drop of the sauce.

COCONUT GREEN CURRY MUSSELS

CURRY BASE

4 cups (1 L) high-fat coconut milk

½ yellow onion, sliced

2 cloves garlic, sliced

1 stalk lemongrass, sliced

2-inch (5 cm) piece galangal,
   peeled and sliced

2-inch (5 cm) piece ginger, peeled
   and sliced

3 lime leaves, sliced into thin strips

3 Tbsp (45 mL) Thai green curry
   paste

1 bunch cilantro, chopped

1 bunch green onion, cut in 2-inch
   (5 cm) pieces

Lime juice to taste

Fish sauce to taste

Sambal oelek or sriracha sauce
   (optional)

MUSSELS

1 cup (250 mL) chicken stock

5 lb (2.2 kg) Salt Spring Island or
   Gallo mussels

SERVES 4 TO 6

PREPARE THE CURRY BASE: Skim 4 Tbsp (60 mL) pure coconut fat from the top of the coconut milk and add it to a medium-size pot.

Over medium heat, bring the coconut fat to a simmer, then stir in the yellow onions, garlic, lemongrass, galangal, ginger, and lime leaves. Mix well. Continue to cook the vegetables in coconut fat until the onions are soft and translucent and the fat starts to separate.

Stir in the green curry paste, making sure to completely coat the vegetable mixture. Cook for 2 to 3 minutes or until the mixture begins to stick to the bottom of the pot. Reduce the heat if necessary.

Add the remaining coconut milk, stirring well, and bring to a gentle simmer. Cook uncovered for 30 minutes or until the curry starts to thicken.

Stir in half of the cilantro and half of the green onions. Simmer for 5 more minutes, season to taste with lime juice and fish sauce, then remove from the heat and strain into a container.

The curry base can be prepared a day ahead to this point. It should be slightly salty, tangy, and spicy; if you like more heat, add some sambal oelek or sriracha sauce.

MAKE THE MUSSELS: In a large pot over medium-high heat, bring the curry base and chicken stock to a simmer. Add the mussels, cover, and cook for 7 to 10 minutes or until they have all opened. Discard any that don't.

Divide the mussels and curry between four to six bowls—or just one big one that everyone can share—and garnish with the remaining cilantro and green onions. Serve with warm or grilled bread.

It isn't a party if there aren't sliders, especially Executive Chef Barr's beef tartare on a bun. They combine the elegance of haute French cuisine with the ease of North American casual fare, all in a bite-size morsel.

MINI BEEF TARTARE BURGERS

BEEF TARTARE

6 oz (170 g) beef sirloin, sinew
    and fat removed
2 tsp (5 g) chopped capers
2 tsp (5 g) chopped pickles
1 tsp (5 mL) Worcestershire sauce
2 tsp (10 mL) Dijon mustard
1 shallot, finely chopped
2 tsp (2 g) finely chopped flat-leaf
    parsley
2 tsp (10 mL) sherry vinegar
2 Tbsp (30 mL) cold-pressed
    canola oil
Couple of dashes Tabasco sauce
Salt and cracked black pepper

ASSEMBLY

4 leaves romaine lettuce
24 slider buns
⅔ cup (160 mL) ketchup
⅔ cup (160 mL) mayonnaise
1 shallot, sliced into fine rings

MAKES 24 SLIDERS

MAKE THE TARTARE: Chop the beef into a very fine dice. Combine with the rest of the ingredients and adjust seasoning as needed.

TO ASSEMBLE: Use a small circle cutter to punch 24 circles slightly bigger than the burger buns out of the lettuce. Apply a touch of ketchup to one side of the buns and mayonnaise to the other. Place a small spoonful of tartare on the bottom bun, then top with shallot rings and lettuce and finish with the top bun.

INN-STYLE

For a more dramatic presentation, Executive Chef Barr serves these sliders on buns housemade from gluten-free cornbread. If you'd like to do the same, use the cornbread recipe on page 70 to make the batter. Preheat the oven to 300°F (150°C). Sprinkle about ½ tsp (1 g) toasted sesame seeds into the bottom of 2-inch (5 cm) silicone dome moulds, then spoon in some batter so that the moulds are not quite full. Bake until golden and a wooden skewer inserted into the centre comes out clean, about 15 to 20 minutes. Cool completely before topping with tartare and accompaniments as above.

"The Wick raised the bar for all future Relais & Châteaux property conferences."

Chef Profile: ANDREW SPRINGETT

IN NOVEMBER 2003, Andrew Springett joined the Inn as chef de cuisine. "I was recommended by Rod 'the God' Butters for the first chef's position," he recalls. Chef Springett's very first menu featured what he still considers his most memorable dish, the foie gras and smoked salmon terrine with caviar. "I believe it achieved the level of food expected at a Relais & Châteaux property," he says now.

His favourite memory of the three and a half years he spent at the Inn was the Relais & Châteaux conference. "It was one of the biggest and most important events held by the property and one of the biggest events experienced by me as a chef," he says. "The comments by the guests were how the Wick raised the bar for all future Relais & Châteaux property conferences."

Today, after a few years spent cooking at Black Rock Oceanfront Resort in Ucluelet, Chef Springett is a chef-instructor at the Southern Alberta Institute of Technology (SAIT) in Calgary. It was working at the Inn that forced him to mature as a chef, he says, especially the "blue sky" meetings with management that allowed him to imagine all sorts of exciting ideas and possibilities.

"It was the hardest, most rewarding job I have had," Chef Springett says. "Visiting the property, post-employment, gave me an opportunity to see the Wick from a guest point of view. The word 'magical' has been used. The place creates an experience like no other."

◀ *Chef Springett's Sweet English Pea Soup with Seared Scallops and Buttered Leeks (recipe on page 152)*

From the Sea

▼

SEAFOOD

> **The Inn's chefs have always known the Pacific Ocean is precious and needs protection. Sustainability has always been on the menu.**

JUST BEYOND THE doors of the Wickaninnish Inn rolls the vast Pacific Ocean, its deep greeny-blue depths alive with a sumptuous buffet of sea life. Just ask any chef who has spent time in the Inn's kitchens: this is paradise for seafood lovers.

From the day the Inn opened its doors, the Pacific has been the Inn's very own grocery store. It teems with fish—fresh, flavourful, and sustainable. There is salmon, of course, all five of British Columbia's indigenous species, including the precious sockeye, with its deep-red flesh and succulent flavour. Salmon appears at every meal: cured, smoked, grilled, pan-fried, poached, roasted, or even tucked inside a macaron. And there is halibut, its sturdy white flesh a perfect foil for intense sauces, and albacore tuna, best served lightly seared and tickled with delicate Asian spices. Sometimes there is sablefish, trout, rockfish or octopus.

There are also shellfish here: beds of oysters, clams, scallops, and mussels that are showcased in our soups and chowders. There are giant beach oysters, so large it takes two hands to hold one, and the precious gooseneck barnacles only the most intrepid of fishermen can harvest from wave-swept rocks. Shrimp abound in these waters, too, the buttery spot prawn with its all-too-short season and the plentiful sweet side-stripe or humpback shrimp. Sometimes octopus and squid make their way onto the menu, as well as sea urchins and the giant clams that look so disreputable, but taste so good.

Perhaps the most distinctively local seafood is the Dungeness crab. In these waters it's in season year-round, at once a rare delicacy and an everyday comfort food. Many Tofitians will just boil a crab in salt water and then crack its claws, picking out the sweet meat and dipping it in melted butter. But the Inn's chefs can think of many other ways to serve it: as crab cakes (page 111) or in pasta (page 144), on eggs benny, or in potlatch (page 126).

The ocean may seem like an endless seafood buffet, but the Inn's chefs have always known that it is precious and needs protection. Sustainability has always been on the menu along with the smoked salmon and crab cakes. Luckily, here it's easy to find seafood choices that are as environmentally friendly as they are good to eat.

In the early days, Chef Butters's "potlatch" was one of the most-talked-about dishes on the menu. "Potlatch was my version of a completely 100 percent local seafood bouillabaisse," he says. This glorious stew makes the most of local seafood and is inspired by the traditions of the west coast First Nations. The traditional potlatch was a feast celebrated by the Haida and Coast Salish peoples and involved elaborate rituals, gifts, and, of course, food from the sea. (The word "potlatch" comes from a Nuu-chah-nulth word that means "to give away.") Not all of these delicacies are widely available; we recommend you either substitute with what is in your region or increase the amount of the ingredients that you do have available. Chef Butters also suggests making the tomato-vegetable base ahead of time to allow the flavours to mingle and advises you will need a large covered casserole dish.

POTLATCH

TOMATO-VEGETABLE STEW

¼ cup (60 mL) grapeseed oil

1 medium onion, diced

4 cloves garlic, finely chopped

1 cup (100 g) diced celeriac

1 bulb fennel, diced

1 small zucchini, diced

6 green onions, diced

1 large parsnip, peeled and diced

½ cup (125 mL) tomato paste

2 cups (400 mL) chopped plum
    tomatoes, canned or fresh

½ cup (30 g) chopped mixed
    herbs, such as dill, basil, and
    cilantro

1 Tbsp (15 mL) Worcestershire
    sauce

½ tsp (1 g) chili flakes

1 Tbsp (15 mL) balsamic vinegar

Sea salt and cracked black pepper
    to taste

Photo on page 52

MAKE THE TOMATO-VEGETABLE STEW: In a large pot over medium heat, heat the grapeseed oil. Add the onions and garlic and cook until soft. Add the celeriac, fennel, zucchini, green onions, and parsnip and cook for 3 to 5 minutes until soft; do not allow to brown.

Stir in the tomato paste and cook until the bottom of the pot gets a bit sticky. Add all of the remaining ingredients. Stir and scrape the bottom of the pot. Reduce the heat to a low simmer and cook for 30 minutes. Adjust the seasoning to taste. The stew can be used immediately or made up to 2 days ahead of time and chilled until needed.

ASSEMBLE THE POTLATCH: Preheat the oven to 375°F (190°C).

In a skillet over medium heat, heat the olive oil, then add the sliced red onions. Cook until soft, then spread evenly in the bottom of a large deep-sided casserole dish or Dutch oven.

Arrange all the seafood on top of the onions in the casserole dish—layer fish on the bottom and top with shelled shellfish, then with larger shells, and finally with the smallest shellfish.

Ladle the tomato-vegetable stew on top, ensuring the seafood is completely covered. Sprinkle with herbs and salt and pepper. Cover with the lid and place on the bottom rack in the oven.

Bake for 20 to 30 minutes or until the seafood is cooked through. All the shells should have opened; discard any unopened clams or mussels. Divide between four bowls and serve with warm, crusty sourdough bread.

POTLATCH

2 Tbsp (30 mL) olive oil

1 medium red onion, thinly sliced

1 lb (450 g) fresh fish (use a variety), cut into 2-inch (5 cm) cubes

4 crab legs

8 pink in-shell swimming scallops

4 medium oysters, shelled

4 large scallops, shelled

8 spot prawns, with or without shells

6 oz (170 g) octopus, cut in thin strips

12 mussels, rinsed well in cold water, any opened shells discarded

12 clams, rinsed well in cold water, any opened shells discarded

12 gooseneck barnacles (optional)

5 cups (1.25 L) tomato-vegetable stew (recipe opposite)

¼ cup (15 g) chopped mixed herbs

Sea salt and cracked black pepper to taste

SERVES 4

Inspired by a classic Japanese dish, Chef Ly balances tender local tuna with savoury umami flavours and the toothsome bite of wakame. Wakame is a type of seaweed that is becoming a culinary darling for its sustainability and powerful nutrients. It makes a perfect partner for the sustainable albacore tuna from the waters off Vancouver Island, especially when tossed with flavours of ginger and sesame. Best of all, all the components of this dish can be made ahead of time and easily assembled at a moment's notice.

SEARED ALBACORE TUNA with
MARINATED SHIITAKE MUSHROOMS and WAKAME SALAD

MARINATED MUSHROOMS

¾ cup (185 mL) soy sauce
1 cup (250 mL) mirin
¼ cup (60 mL) rice wine vinegar
½ cup (125 mL) sake
12 whole dehydrated shiitake
   mushrooms

ASIAN DRESSING

¼ cup (60 mL) soy sauce
2 Tbsp (30 mL) mirin
2 Tbsp (30 mL) rice wine vinegar
2 Tbsp (30 mL) sake
1 Tbsp (15 mL) lime juice
1 Tbsp (5 g) finely chopped ginger
¼ cup (60 mL) canola oil
1½ Tbsp (22 mL) sesame oil
Salt and cracked black pepper

ASSEMBLY

1 package dried wakame
   (seaweed)
12 oz (340 g) albacore tuna loin
Salt and cracked black pepper to
   taste
Toasted sesame seeds (optional)
Thai chili, chopped (optional)

SERVES 2 TO 4

Photo on page 192

THE NIGHT BEFORE, PREPARE THE MARINATED MUSHROOMS: In a small saucepan, combine the soy sauce, mirin, rice wine vinegar, and sake and bring to a boil. Place the mushrooms in a small heatproof bowl and pour the marinade over them. Allow them to rehydrate overnight. If necessary, weight the mushrooms so they are fully submerged.

Make the Asian dressing: In a small bowl, combine all the ingredients, except the salt and pepper, and whisk together. Season to taste with salt and pepper.

TO ASSEMBLE: In a heatproof bowl, place the wakame. Bring a pot of water just to a boil and pour over the wakame, letting it sit until it is rehydrated, about 5 minutes. Drain and refresh in a bowl of ice water, then drain again. Toss with about half the Asian dressing and set aside.

Season the tuna with salt and pepper. Bring a sauté pan to high heat, then sear the tuna for about 10 seconds per side; it should still be rare inside. Slice into 12 thin slices.

Slice the mushrooms into thin pieces and divide between two plates for a main course or four plates for a starter. Shingle the tuna over the mushrooms, then top the tuna with wakame salad. Drizzle the remaining Asian dressing around the plates. If you like, garnish with sesame seeds and chopped Thai chilies.

This dramatic dish is one of Executive Chef Barr's signatures. The oysters are battered in leek ash to look like coals, a crisp black crust enfolding the tender, briny shellfish. The pristine waters around Vancouver Island produce some of the world's best oysters, including the plump beach oysters this recipe calls for. This dish is designed to impress.

OYSTER COALS

LEEK ASH
4 leeks, green parts only

BLACK GARLIC MARINADE
2 heads garlic
2 tsp (10 mL) olive oil
2 heads black garlic
1 cup (250 mL) water
½ tsp (2 mL) honey

OYSTERS
18 medium beach oysters
1 cup (170 g) potato starch or
    1 cup (130 g) corn starch
8 cups (2 L) canola oil, or as
    needed

CUMIN AIOLI
2 Tbsp (30 mL) lemon juice
2 Tbsp (30 mL) white wine
    vinegar
2 egg yolks
½ Tbsp (3 g) cumin seeds
½ tsp (1 g) espelette pepper
1 cup (250 mL) cumin oil
    (page 259)
Salt to taste

SERVES 4 TO 6

MAKE THE LEEK ASH: Preheat the oven to 400°F (200°C). Chop and wash the leek greens thoroughly. Dry them well and divide between two baking sheets lined with silicone liners, spreading them out evenly. Bake until the leeks turn black but still have a slight nose of leek, about 1 hour. Remove from the oven, cool, then place in a blender and grind into a fine powder.

MAKE THE BLACK GARLIC MARINADE: To roast the garlic, preheat the oven to 350°F (180°C). Trim the tops off the garlic, then lay the heads on a sheet of aluminum foil. Drizzle with the olive oil, then wrap the foil around them. Bake in the oven for 30 to 35 minutes or until soft. Allow to cool, then peel the roasted garlic and the black garlic. In a blender or food processor, place both garlics, the water, honey, and 2 Tbsp (15 g) of the leek ash and purée until very smooth.

MARINATE THE OYSTERS: Turn the oven up to 450°F (230°C). Place the oysters on a baking sheet and bake for 4 minutes. Once the oysters are cool enough to handle, shuck them into a strainer and remove any bits of shell. (Alternatively, you can use pre-shucked oysters, provided they are fairly big and exceptionally fresh.) Toss them in the black garlic marinade, making sure they are fully coated, and refrigerate overnight to marinate.

PREPARE THE CUMIN AIOLI: In a blender or food processor, combine all the ingredients except the cumin oil and salt. While the machine is running, drizzle in the oil until thick and emulsified. Season to taste with salt.

COOK THE OYSTERS: Mix ⅔ cup (64 g) of the leek ash with the potato or corn starch. Toss the oysters in the mixture until well coated.
    In a deep, heavy-bottomed pot, heat the oil to 350°F (180°C). Use a thermometer to ensure the right temperature. In batches of six, fry the oysters until dark and crispy. Serve immediately with cumin aioli.

For sheer beauty, little can compete with this dish, one of Executive Chef Barr's signatures. Local salmon is cured, dusted with powdered seaweed, then pressed into a sophisticated mosaic-like pattern. Chef Barr uses local bull kelp, which washes up on Chesterman Beach in mighty tangles, but if it's not available to you, you could use another dried seaweed; several varieties are available online and in Asian markets.

SALMON MOSAIC

SALMON MOSAIC

1 lb (450 g) salt

16 cups (4 L) water

1 fillet sockeye salmon, 4 lb
    (1.8 kg)

1 oz (30 g) dried bull kelp powder,
    plus additional for garnish

Canola oil, as needed

1 cucumber

1 small daikon

Salt to taste

1½ Tbsp (20 mL) kelp vinegar
    (page 258)

2 Tbsp (30 mL) dill oil, plus
    additional for garnish
    (page 260)

1 oz (30 g) salmon roe

2 sprigs dill

CULTURED CREAM

⅓ cup (80 mL) buttermilk

1⅔ cups (410 mL) cream

SERVES 4

CURE THE SALMON: In a large pot, bring the salt and water to a boil, then cool to room temperature. Remove the skin and pin bones from the salmon fillet, being sure to remove any blood lines and brown flesh. Cut into lengthwise strips about 1 inch (2.5 cm) wide, then cut in half across the strips. Place the salmon in a wide pan and pour the cool brine over the fish. Leave to brine for 15 minutes in the refrigerator, then remove the fish and pat dry. Arrange the fish on kitchen towels on a tray so that the air can circulate around it, and refrigerate overnight.

The next day, the salmon should have a sticky film on it. Stretch some plastic wrap tightly over a flat tabletop. Dust each strip of salmon generously with the kelp powder.

Stack the salmon strips on the plastic wrap so that you can wrap them up entirely. Carefully and using lots of pressure, shape the salmon stack into a cylinder, wrapping it very tightly with lots of plastic wrap. Stab the cylinder with a cake tester to release any air pockets and continue to shape and tighten the cylinder. Make sure the pressure is coming from the side of the cylinder, not the ends.

When super-tight and firm, place the salmon cylinder in the freezer. The mosaic can be made several days ahead to this point.

Two days before you plan to serve the mosaic, make the cultured cream: Whisk the buttermilk and cream together and transfer to a clean container. Wrap in plastic wrap and leave at room temperature for 2 days—it will become rich, thick, and tangy. Transfer to the fridge until needed.

TO ASSEMBLE THE MOSAIC: Pull the salmon cylinder from the freezer and let it partially thaw, just enough to slice, so you can return the remaining salmon to the freezer. Slice four portions ½ to 1 inch (1 to 2.5 cm) thick, depending on the size of the salmon. Brush each slice with a touch of canola oil for shine.

Using a mandoline, shave long slices of cucumber and daikon and dress with the salt, kelp vinegar, and dill oil. Use the back of a spoon to swirl some cultured cream in the centre of four plates. Place the salmon mosaic in the centre of each plate and garnish to one side with cucumber and daikon. Spoon some salmon roe over the garnish and finish with sprigs of dill. Drizzle the plates with additional dill oil and dust with kelp powder.

This is not your everyday canapé. Executive Chef Barr's savoury-sweet macarons have a shell that hints at pumpernickel and is filled with a creamy smoked salmon layer. Macarons are notoriously tricky to bake, so in this recipe follow the measurements in weight for greatest accuracy. Using an electronic scale is the best way to ensure these delicate biscuits turn out perfectly.

SMOKED SALMON MACARONS

MAKE THE SMOKED SALMON FILLING: In a stand mixer, whip the cream cheese until light and fluffy. Add the salmon and continue to mix. Fold in the remaining ingredients and adjust seasoning as needed.

MAKE THE MACARON SHELLS: Preheat the oven to 275°F (135°C) and line two baking sheets with parchment paper.

Into a medium-size bowl, sift the icing sugar, almond flour, cocoa powder, and salt.

In a stand mixer fitted with a whip attachment, place half the egg whites (35 g).

Place the remaining half of the egg whites (35 g) and coffee grounds in a small bowl and set aside.

In a small pot set over medium heat, stir together the sugar, molasses, and water and attach a candy thermometer to the side. When the syrup reaches 239°F (115°C), start whipping the egg whites in the stand mixer on high.

As the mixer continues to whip the egg whites, once the syrup comes to 244°F (118°C), remove from the heat and slowly pour down the side of the mixing bowl. Continue whipping until the bottom of the bowl is just warm.

Recipe continues ▶

SMOKED SALMON FILLING

⅔ cup (150 g) cream cheese
5 oz (150 g) hot-smoked salmon
1½ Tbsp (13 g) chopped capers
1½ Tbsp (4 g) chopped chives
1½ Tbsp (4 g) chopped dill
Finely grated zest and juice of
 1 lemon

PUMPERNICKEL MACARONS

¾ cup (100 g) icing sugar
1 cup (100 g) almond flour
1⅓ Tbsp (7 g) cocoa powder
½ tsp (2 g) salt
5 Tbsp (70 g) egg whites, about
 2½ eggs, room temperature
½ tsp (1 g) ground coffee
7 Tbsp (85 g) sugar
1 tsp (8 g) molasses
1½ Tbsp (23 g) water
2 to 3 Tbsp (12 to 18 g) caraway
 seeds, toasted
Sea salt

MAKES 20 TO 25 FILLED MACARONS

Pour the liquid egg-white/coffee mixture into the icing-sugar/ almond-flour mixture. Add a third of the beaten egg-white mixture and, using a rubber spatula, mix well until you have a uniform paste. Fold in the rest of the beaten egg-white mixture, a third at a time, mixing well before adding the next round.

Scoop the macaron batter into a piping bag fitted with a small round tip and shake to remove as many bubbles as possible. Pipe a touch of the batter on the back corners of the pieces of parchment paper and stick them to the baking sheets (this will prevent the parchment from flying up in the oven), then pipe small rounds of batter directly onto the parchment-lined baking sheets. Tap the baking sheets a few times to remove any bubbles from the macaron shells. If any of the macaron rounds have pointy centres, flatten them with a moistened fingertip.

Sprinkle with the toasted caraway seeds and a touch of sea salt.

Leaving the oven door slightly open to allow any moisture to escape, bake for 5 minutes, then rotate the baking sheets. Bake for another 5 minutes, then check doneness by jiggling the macarons. If they are still jiggly and not set on their feet, bake another minute or two. Remove from the oven and cool completely.

Use a piping bag to apply the smoked salmon mousse to the flat side of a macaron, then place another macaron on top to form a little sandwich. Repeat with the remaining macarons.

Salmon is the king of the west coast, its tender, pink flesh prized by chefs and diners alike. Wild salmon is both sustainable and delicious, and at the Inn, Chef Springett served it in a dish that was at once simple and complex: alongside the salmon and bean ragout, he'd offer a sliced scallop sausage (as shown here; recipe on page 153) and mixed green salad. At home, you can, of course, prepare this any way you like.

Lemon-Basted SALMON with WHITE BEAN RAGOUT

WHITE BEAN RAGOUT

1 cup (200 g) dried white beans, such as great northern or cannellini

2 carrots, peeled and diced large

4 stalks celery, diced large

2 bay leaves

¼ cup (60 mL) grapeseed oil

2 shallots, finely diced

¼ cup (20 g) halved (lengthwise) and thinly sliced well-washed leeks

1½ cups (375 mL) cream

1 tsp (5 mL) Dijon mustard

Salt and cayenne pepper to taste

4 Tbsp (35 g) candied salmon, diced (page 105)

2 Tbsp (30 g) butter

Lemon juice to taste

Chopped chives to taste

SALMON

¼ cup (60 mL) grapeseed oil

4 fillets spring or coho salmon, 6 oz (170 g) each, skin on

2 Tbsp (30 g) butter

2 sprigs thyme

2 cloves garlic, skin on, crushed

2 wedges lemon

ASSEMBLY

Oven-roasted cherry tomatoes (optional)

Herb Scallop Sausage (page 153), sliced

SERVES 4

MAKE THE WHITE BEAN RAGOUT: Soak the beans at room temperature overnight by placing them in a large bowl with enough water to cover them by at least 2 inches (5 cm). Do not add salt.

The next day, drain and rinse the beans, then place them in a pot with the carrots, celery, and bay leaves. Add cold unsalted water to cover them and simmer until tender, adding more water if needed, about 1½ hours. Drain and set aside; these can be done a day ahead to this point.

In a small pot, bring the oil to medium heat and sweat the shallots and leeks until tender. Add the beans, cream, and mustard. Lightly season with salt and cayenne, then simmer until the cream has reduced enough to coat the beans. Remove from the heat, fold in the candied salmon and butter, and season with lemon juice, chives, and more salt and cayenne to taste.

PREPARE THE SALMON: Heat a stainless steel pan to medium-high heat, add the oil, and bring to a light smoke point, then place the salmon in the pan flesh side down. Cook until lightly browned, then flip the fish to skin side down and lower the heat to medium. Cook the salmon until just warm inside; this should take about 5 minutes. When done, remove from the heat and add the butter, thyme, garlic, and lemon wedges to the pan. Baste the salmon with the seasoned, melted butter.

TO SERVE: Divide the bean ragout between four plates and place a piece of salmon on top of each. If you like, you can top with oven-roasted cherry tomatoes, and serve with slices of scallop sausage.

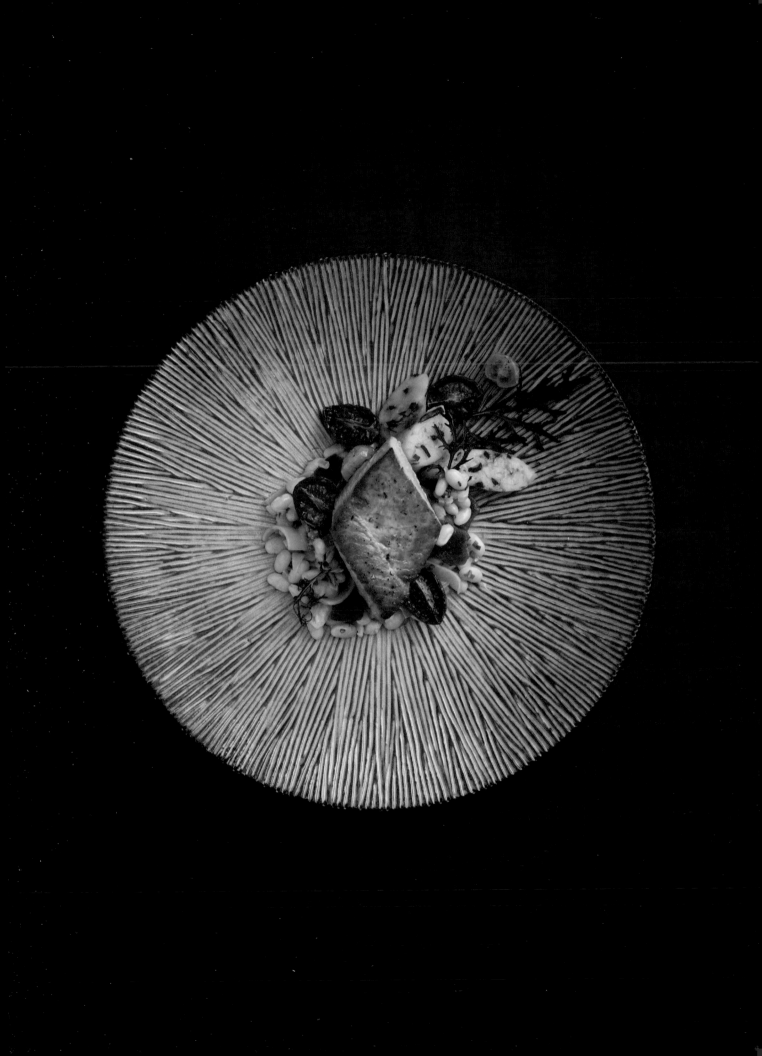

British Columbia is famous for its salmon, but should be just as renowned for its halibut. Some of the best comes from Haida Gwaii, the archipelago north of Vancouver Island. Although halibut has a very mild flavour, Chef Butters discovered that its firm flesh stands up nicely to hearty sauces like this chunky, tangy mixture based on a classic gribiche.

Haida Gwaii HALIBUT and ASPARAGUS

DRESSING

2 hard-boiled eggs, peeled and sliced

1 large dill pickle, diced

2 strips bacon, diced and cooked

1 Tbsp (5 g) chopped flat-leaf parsley

1 Tbsp (15 mL) olive oil

HALIBUT

3 to 4 Tbsp (45 g to 60 g) butter

2 fillets halibut, 6 oz (170 g) each

Sea salt and cracked black pepper

2 cloves garlic, cut into slivers

1 lb (450 g) asparagus, tough bottoms of spears removed

SERVES 2

MAKE THE DRESSING: In a small bowl, combine all the ingredients. Keep at room temperature until ready to serve.

MAKE THE HALIBUT: Heat a skillet, preferably non-stick, on medium heat. Add the butter to the pan.

Season the halibut with salt and pepper. When the butter is hot and foamy, place the halibut in the pan and cook on one side until a golden-brown crust develops.

Turn the fish over and cook on the other side until done, adjusting the heat higher or lower if necessary. Add the garlic slivers just before the fish is done. Cooking time should be 6 to 10 minutes, depending on the thickness of the fish; the flesh should still be a little translucent in the middle when done. Remove the pan from the heat.

While the fish is cooking, bring a pan of water to a boil. Just as the fish finishes cooking, drop the asparagus in the water and cook until it turns bright green—this should take only a few seconds. Remove the asparagus from the boiling water immediately. (Alternatively, you can steam or grill the asparagus.)

Divide the asparagus between two plates. Spoon the egg mixture on top of the asparagus. Place the halibut on top and spoon the garlic pan juices over the fish.

Halibut caught in the waters off British Columbia's west coast is among the world's greatest seafood delicacies. With a mild taste but sturdy texture, it pairs beautifully with a wide range of flavours. Here Chef Ly keeps the seasonings simple to highlight the beauty of the fish, but serves it with an earthy risotto rich with wild mushrooms and creamy avocado. Take care not to overcook the halibut—it takes only seconds to go from perfectly done to dry and disappointing.

Pan-Seared HALIBUT with AVOCADO RISOTTO

RISOTTO

4 cups (1 L) chicken stock
2 Tbsp (30 mL) olive oil
1 small onion, diced small
1 cup (200 g) uncooked arborio rice
½ cup (35 g) chopped fresh morels (or dried and reconstituted with hot water)
1 avocado, diced
2 Tbsp (30 g) butter
¼ cup (25 g) grated Parmesan cheese, or to taste
1 Tbsp (3 g) chopped chives
Salt and cracked black pepper

HALIBUT

1 Tbsp (15 mL) olive oil, plus additional for garnish
4 fillets fresh halibut, 5 oz (140 g) each
Salt and cracked black pepper

SERVES 4

Preheat the oven to 350°F (180°C).

Make the risotto: In a small pot, bring the stock to a simmer and keep it hot while you cook the risotto.

In an 8-cup (2 L) saucepan over medium heat, heat the olive oil. Add the onions and cook until they are tender and translucent; continue cooking for 5 minutes. Add the rice and stir to coat with the oil and onion mixture. Continue cooking for about 3 minutes or until the rice is opaque.

Stir ½ cup (125 mL) of the hot chicken stock into the rice mixture. Cook and stir until the broth is absorbed, maintaining the rice mixture at a gentle simmer. Continue cooking and adding the remaining stock, ½ cup (125 mL) at a time, stirring the rice mixture after each addition.

After about 15 minutes, stir in the mushrooms and continue cooking for another 10 minutes, still adding stock whenever it begins to look dry, until the stock has all been absorbed. The rice should be cooked but still firm in texture. Stir in the avocado, butter, cheese, and chives. Season with salt and pepper to taste.

In the last few minutes of cooking time for the risotto, prepare the halibut: In a 12-inch (30 cm) ovenproof skillet over medium-high heat, heat the oil. Season the halibut fillets with salt and pepper. Place the halibut fillets in the skillet and cook for about 4 to 5 minutes or until the halibut is golden brown.

Using a spatula, flip the halibut fillets over and place in the oven, still in the skillet. Continue cooking for about 4 more minutes or until the halibut is cooked. The fish should flake easily when pressed with a fork, but should still be slightly translucent in the centre.

Divide the risotto between four dinner plates. Top the risotto with the halibut and drizzle the plate with some olive oil.

In Clayoquot Sound, Dungeness crabs are in season year-round, making them a delicacy that can be enjoyed any time in a crab boil, on a salad, or in a more decadent dish. Here Chef Labossiere tucks sweet crabmeat inside pillows of saffron-scented pasta ravioli for an unforgettably luxurious feast.

DUNGENESS CRAB and MASCARPONE RAVIOLI in SAFFRON PASTA

SAFFRON PASTA DOUGH

½ cup (125 mL) water

1 large pinch saffron threads

2 cups (250 g) flour

1 egg

2 egg yolks

Egg wash: 1 egg lightly beaten
   with 1 tsp (5 mL) water

CRAB FILLING

2 Tbsp (30 g) butter

1 leek, white part only, washed
   and julienned

1 shallot, finely chopped

½ lb (225 g) Dungeness crabmeat

5 oz (140 g) mascarpone cheese

2 Tbsp (5 g) chopped chives

1 Tbsp (15 mL) finely chopped or
   puréed black truffles (optional)

Finely grated zest and juice of
   1 lemon

ASSEMBLY

Good-quality olive oil or melted
   butter

Fine sea salt to taste

Pecorino romano or Grana
   Padano cheese, for garnish

SERVES 4

Photo on page 154

MAKE THE SAFFRON PASTA DOUGH: In a small pot, bring the water to a boil. Place the saffron in a small bowl and pour the water overtop to cover. Steep until the liquid cools to room temperature. Stir once and strain.

Place the flour in the bowl of a stand mixer fitted with a dough hook. With the mixer on low speed, add the egg and then the egg yolks one by one, mixing well, then slowly add the saffron tea, mixing until the dough starts to form. It should still be slightly dry at this point.

Increase the speed to medium and mix for 5 to 7 minutes or until a firm ball of dough forms; add more flour or more water if needed. The surface of the dough should be smooth and springy to the touch. Remove from the bowl and set aside to rest until needed, at least 30 minutes.

Once the pasta dough has rested, put it through a pasta roller set at its widest measure. Fold over three times and repeat this step three times. This will strengthen the dough and give it a better texture.

After the final fold, continue putting the dough through the roller at ever thinner settings until it reaches ¹⁄₁₆ inch (2 mm) thick. Lightly flour and cover with a towel until you're ready to assemble the ravioli. Note: The pasta sheet should be the width of the pasta roller at this point.

PREPARE THE CRAB FILLING: In a small pan over medium heat, melt the butter. Add the julienned leeks and finely chopped shallots and cook until soft and translucent. Remove from the heat and cool to room temperature.

In a small bowl, stir the leek mixture together with the crabmeat, mascarpone, chives, and the truffles, if using. Season with the lemon zest and juice.

MAKE THE RAVIOLI: Lightly flour the pasta sheet and roll one more time through the roller (it will have thickened a bit as it rested). Cut the sheet into two equal parts and set one aside—this one will be the top.

Spoon out small rounds of crab filling, about an inch (2.5 cm) in diameter and 2 inches (5 cm) apart, onto the bottom sheet.

Brush the sheet and rounds of filling with egg wash. Gently place the second sheet of pasta overtop. Working from left to right, and using your hands, gently press any air out as you form the shape of the ravioli. Cut out the ravioli with a round cutter or, if you prefer a more rustic pasta, cut into squares with a knife.

Bring a large pot of salted water to a boil. Carefully drop the ravioli into the water and cook for 1 to 2 minutes. They will rise to the top when they are done.

Using a skimmer, remove the ravioli from the water. Divide between four plates, drizzle with a little olive oil or melted butter, and sprinkle with sea salt and cheese. Serve immediately.

INN-STYLE

You can keep this recipe simple and serve it as above, or prepare it the way Chef Labossiere has done in the photo on page 154. Make a carrot purée by simmering chopped carrots in light cream with a bay leaf and a pinch of salt until tender, about 20 minutes, then remove the bay leaf and purée the carrots in a blender. Render some diced guanciale (cured pork jowl) or double-smoked bacon over medium heat until crispy, about 10 minutes, then sautée tiny chanterelle mushrooms and diced carrots and celery root in the pork fat until tender. Season with salt and lemon juice. To serve: Spoon the carrot purée on a plate, top with the vegetables, stack the ravioli on the vegetables, and sprinkle with chopped Italian parsley and grated pecorino cheese.

For a few brief weeks in May, the elusive spot prawn comes into season and the West Coast goes wild for the sweet, buttery crustaceans. Luckily, that tiny window coincides with squash-blossom season. Here Executive Chef Barr's seasonal recipe marries the two unforgettably.

SQUASH BLOSSOMS Stuffed with SPOT PRAWNS

MOUSSE AND SQUASH BLOSSOMS

½ lb (225 g) scallops

Salt

2 egg yolks

⅔ cup (160 mL) whipping cream

1 lb (450 g) spot prawns, peeled

1 shallot, finely chopped

Finely grated zest of 1 lemon

Lemon juice to taste

18 squash blossoms

PESTO

1 clove garlic, finely chopped

2 Tbsp (20 g) pumpkin seeds

Finely grated zest of 1 lemon

¼ cup (25 g) grated pecorino
    romano cheese

¼ cup (60 mL) canola oil

2 ice cubes

1 bunch basil, leaves only

Salt and cracked black pepper to
    taste

ASSEMBLY

1 zucchini

Salt

Lemon juice

Crème fraîche (page 275)

12 reserved spot prawns

1 sprig basil, leaves only, torn

3 Tbsp (25 g) roughly chopped
    pumpkin seeds

SERVES 6

MAKE THE MOUSSE: Make sure the scallops, egg yolks, cream, and prawns are well chilled; also chill the food-processor bowl and blade before using.

Place the scallops and a pinch of salt in the chilled food processor and purée until smooth. Add the egg yolks and continue to process, then add the cream and process until the mousse is silky.

Set aside 12 spot prawns and reserve for later.

Chop the remaining prawns. In a medium-size bowl, mix the chopped prawns with the scallop mousse, shallots, and lemon zest. Season the mixture with salt and lemon juice.

STUFF THE SQUASH BLOSSOMS: Place the mixture into a disposable piping bag and fill each squash blossom so that they are plump but not overflowing. Place on a tray and set in the fridge.

MAKE THE PESTO: In a blender or food processor, blend everything except the basil, salt, and pepper. When well blended, add the basil, then season with salt and pepper. Chill in the fridge with plastic wrap pressed against the surface of the pesto to keep it from going brown.

Using a mandoline, slice the zucchini into thin coins, about ⅛ inch (3 mm) thick. Season with salt and lemon juice.

On six plates, swirl some crème fraîche into a wide circle. Distribute some basil pesto on and around the crème fraîche.

Heat a grill to high. Lightly char the stuffed squash blossoms on all sides, then leave to rest; they should be firm when pressure is applied. Arrange them on the crème fraîche.

Season the remaining prawns with salt and grill them lightly until they are firm but still slightly translucent. Season them with lemon juice and arrange two on each plate. Garnish with torn basil leaves, zucchini slices, and chopped pumpkin seeds.

Raven sculptures on Chesterman Beach ▶

Spot prawns, with their buttery flavour and fleeting availability, are the rock stars of west coast seafood. Less well known are their slightly smaller cousins, the sidestripe shrimp, which surely deserve much greater renown than they currently have. They're among the biggest and most sustainable shrimp, with a sweet flavour and firm texture. They abound along this coast. Here Chef Filatow marinates them for a perfectly simple and delicious light lunch.

SIDESTRIPE SHRIMP ESCABECHE

12 large sidestripe shrimp (16/20 count), shelled, cleaned, and deveined
1 Tbsp (10 g) peeled and finely chopped shallots
¼ cup (60 mL) red wine vinegar
1 sprig tarragon
1 sprig dill
¼ cup (60 mL) olive oil
Sea salt
Handful of baby greens (arugula, kale, beet greens, etc.)
20 sweet cherry tomatoes, halved
2 mini cucumbers, sliced
1 radish, sliced
Crusty bread

SERVES 2

Fill a large bowl with ice water. Bring to a boil a pot of salted water big enough to fit all the shrimp. Dunk the shrimp in the boiling water; immediately remove them and plunge them into ice water for 2 minutes until they are well chilled. Remove and reserve in the refrigerator.

Soak the finely chopped shallots in the vinegar for 30 minutes, then mix in the tarragon, dill, and olive oil to make a marinade. Season with salt. Toss the shrimp with the dressing, then marinate in the refrigerator for 1 hour.

Divide the baby greens between two plates.

Remove the shrimp from the marinade and arrange on top of the baby greens. Toss the tomatoes, cucumbers, and radishes with the dressing, then spoon the vegetables over and around the shrimp and spoon the remaining dressing on top. Serve with crusty bread.

This dish is pure spring in a bowl, making the most of delicate scallops and sweet, tender peas. When Chef Springett served it, for a dramatic presentation he would place the leek mixture in a soup spoon with the scallop on top garnished with peashoots and chives, and place the spoon in a hot but otherwise empty soup plate. A server would bring the plate to the table and pour the pea soup into the bowl tableside. Bravo!

SWEET ENGLISH PEA SOUP with SEARED SCALLOPS and BUTTERED LEEKS

PEA SOUP

⅓ cup (80 mL) grapeseed oil

2 medium shallots, thinly sliced

½ leek, white part only, thinly sliced

½ cup (125 mL) dry white vermouth

4 cups (1 L) chicken or vegetable stock

Salt and cayenne pepper to taste

2 lb (900 g) English peas, fresh or frozen

½ cup (125 mL) cream

2 oz (60 g) spinach, leaves only (optional)

SCALLOPS

2 Tbsp (30 g) butter

1 shallot, thinly sliced

½ leek, white part only, thinly sliced

Salt to taste

4 to 12 large scallops, abductor muscles removed

Peashoots, chives, and chive flowers, for garnish

SERVES 4

Make the soup: Heat a large stainless steel pot over medium heat, add the grapeseed oil, then add the shallots and leeks and sweat until translucent; do not allow to brown.

Add the vermouth and continue cooking over medium heat until the liquid is reduced by half, about 10 minutes. Add the stock and bring to a simmer. Check seasonings; if necessary, adjust with salt and cayenne. Add the peas and cream and bring to a boil. Cook until the peas are soft, about 10 minutes.

Place in a blender or food processor and purée until smooth. Optional: If you'd like a more intense green colour, add the spinach leaves now and purée until fine. Strain through a sieve to remove any solid bits. Place back into a cleaned pot and bring to a simmer. Adjust seasonings if necessary and keep warm until ready to serve.

Meanwhile, in a sauté pan over medium heat, heat 1 Tbsp (15 g) butter, then sweat the shallots and leeks until tender but not browned. Season with a little salt, remove from the pan, and set aside.

Turn the heat up and add the remaining tablespoon of butter to the pan. Pat the scallops dry, then sear them in the butter, turning them once. This should not take more than a minute or two—you want them to be medium-cooked at most.

Divide the leek mixture among four warmed soup plates, mounding it in the centre of each. Balance a seared scallop (or more, depending on how many you have cooked) on top of the leek mixture. Pour the pea soup around the garnish so the scallops look like they are floating in a pool of green. Garnish with the peashoots, chives, and chive flowers.

Light and delicate, this scallop sausage makes a delicious side, the way Chef Springett served it with his seared salmon and bean ragout (page 138). But it would also make a great addition to a seafood charcuterie board or part of a gourmet brunch. You can buy sausage casings from traditional butchers who make their own sausages, or order them online.

HERB SCALLOP SAUSAGE

If you are using sausage casings, rinse them thoroughly before you start. Also chill all the ingredients before you start.

Fold all the ingredients together, then cook a small amount (about 1 tsp/5 mL) to check for seasoning. Adjust salt and cayenne if needed.

Pipe the filling into sausage casings or plastic wrap and wrap tightly. Prepare an ice bath—a large bowl or pan of water and ice. Bring a pot of water to 185°F (85°C) and gently place the sausages in the simmering water. Poach for 5 minutes, then use a skimmer to remove them and place them in the ice bath to cool. The sausages can be made a day ahead to this point.

TO SERVE: If you've used sausage casings, sear the sausages in grapeseed oil before serving. If you've used plastic wrap, place back into a 185°F (85°C) bath for 3 minutes to warm.

4 sausage casings, preferably lamb, 8 inches (20 cm) each, or plastic wrap

10 oz (300 g) fresh scallops, abductor muscles removed and scallops finely diced

½ tsp (0.5 g) finely chopped dill

½ tsp (0.5 g) finely chopped flat-leaf parsley

4 Tbsp (35 g) diced red bell peppers

1 egg white

Salt and cayenne pepper to taste

Grapeseed oil for searing

MAKES 4 SAUSAGES

On Chesterman Beach, Chef Labossiere fell in love both with cooking and his wife to be. "I will cherish both for the rest of my life."

Chef Profile: JUSTIN LABOSSIERE

IN 2000, JUSTIN LABOSSIERE was a dishwasher at the Inn when one night the garde manger—the cook responsible for appetizers and cold dishes—didn't show up for his shift. "It was busy and the chef had me throw on my whites and said, 'That's a frying pan and that's a scallop.' I felt in that moment like I was the scallop going into the frying pan! At the end of the night he offered me the job."

Chef Labossiere had grown up on Vancouver Island eating sockeye salmon, fresh-picked chanterelles, and giant beach oysters roasted over an open fire. But it was working at the Inn that really got him to appreciate and respect where he was from.

Over two years, he graduated from garde manger to entremetier, the cook responsible for soups and the Inn's famous chowders. His favourite dish, though, was Dungeness crab and mascarpone ravioli. "This was my first time really falling in love with food that wasn't my mother's cooking," he says. "I remember eating it that first time and can still taste it." There on Chesterman Beach, Chef Labossiere fell in love both with cooking and his wife to be. "I will cherish both for the rest of my life."

Today, after working in several roles, including executive chef at Calgary's NOtaBLE the Restaurant, he is the culinary director, national brand, for Calgary's Concorde Entertainment Group. "Without that chance of having to work the line in the most difficult of times I would never have become a chef," he says. "The Wick instilled my absolute love and passion for cooking. To this day it is still the shining example of professionalism and leadership for me."

◀ *Chef Labossiere's Dungeness Crab and Mascarpone Ravioli in Saffron Pasta (recipe on page 144)*

From the Land

▼

MEAT, POULTRY, AND VEGETABLES

THE RAINFOREST ALONG this coast is deep and velvety with silence. Mist wreaths through the branches of ancient cedars and Sitka spruce. Trails wind through the woods, past tree trunks fringed with soft green moss, leading to sandy beaches and rocky hilltops with endless ocean views. Amid the grey-green leaves of low-lying bushes peek flashes of colour: red huckleberries, blue Oregon grapes, orange salmonberries, dark purple cynamokas. Tucked amid the tree roots, nearly hidden by scattered leaves and moss, are the wild mushrooms, including chanterelles, king boletes, and pines, while chicken of the woods grow up the trunks of trees in a lacy frill.

The ocean is not the only source of bounty here. So is the land.

Foragers know just where to find the tender chanterelles and tart cynamokas, citrusy hemlock tips and pleasantly astringent lichens. Buckets and bins of wild edibles appear at the Inn's kitchen door, ready to be transformed by the kitchen brigade. It's a creative challenge for the chefs: What can we do with this? How can we preserve that?

From forest to field, Vancouver Island is a buffet for the discerning diner. It is home to some of Canada's most fertile land, especially in the Comox and Cowichan Valleys, and its mild climate means farmers can grow produce year-round, as long as there's someone to buy it. The Inn gave farmers the customer they needed. As far back as 1996, Chef Butters created a network of suppliers that every succeeding chef has built on. Today, Executive Chef Barr works closely with the Tofino Ucluelet Culinary Guild, which connects growers, chefs, and consumers.

The Pointe, and many other restaurants that followed in Tofino and all over Vancouver Island, gave farmers a steady outlet for their products; the farmers, in turn, were happy to grow the produce the chefs were craving—heirloom carrots, for instance, or baby squash. Now, even without the chefs' skill in transforming the humblest ingredient into something sublime, what comes from Vancouver Island farms is extraordinary. There is heirloom pork, grass-fed bison, and lamb fattened on salty-sweet sea grass. Plump chicken and meaty duck. Sweet tree fruits and earthy root vegetables, leafy greens, and sun-soaked tomatoes. Fresh herbs—basil and thyme, rosemary and lavender, tarragon for French flair, cilantro for an Asian touch. Even truffles, so rare and precious, are grown here and are slowly making their way to chefs' kitchens.

Executive Chef Barr makes it his mission to use as much local product as possible, whether it is from the ocean, the rainforest, or nearby farms. "Our guests should know they are dining on the west coast of Vancouver Island even if it's too dark to see outside," he says. This dish, for instance, uses local mushrooms, hemlock tips, cynamoka berries, and elk—herds of which roam the island. "Even the plating of this dish is meant to be reminiscent of the forest floor at fall," he says.

ELK with FOREST FLAVOURS

ELK AND JUS

2½ lb (1.125 kg) elk loin
2 Tbsp (30 mL) grapeseed oil
2 medium shallots, sliced
2 medium carrots, diced
2 stalks celery, diced
2 cloves garlic, sliced
½ Tbsp (7 mL) tomato paste
2 Tbsp (30 mL) red wine vinegar
1 cup (250 mL) port
4 cups (1 L) red wine
4 cups (1 L) veal jus
4 cups (1 L) chicken stock
2 sprigs thyme
1 tsp (3 g) black peppercorns

CELERIAC BARK, FONDANT, AND PURÉE

2 large celeriac
8 cups (2 L) canola oil
Salt or hemlock salt (page 275)
    to taste
1 cup (230 g) butter
1 sprig thyme
3 cloves garlic, crushed
Juice of 1 lemon
2 cups (500 mL) milk

PREPARE THE ELK AND JUS: Remove any sinew from the elk, then portion the elk into six 5 oz (140 g), evenly shaped pieces, reserving all trim and excess. Dice the trim into small pieces.

In a medium-size pot over medium heat, heat the grapeseed oil. When it's hot, add the elk trimmings and cook until deep brown and caramelized. Stir in the shallots, carrots, celery, and garlic and cook until caramelized. Stir in the tomato paste and cook for another 3 to 4 minutes, then deglaze with the vinegar.

Add the port and red wine and continue cooking, reducing until nearly dry. Add the veal jus, chicken stock, thyme, and peppercorns and reduce to sauce consistency, skimming off any fat that rises to the top. This could take a couple of hours in total.

Meanwhile, prepare the celeriac, starting with the bark: Use a knife to remove the skin and roots from the celeriac so that the remaining celeriac is pure white. Use a mandoline to shave 12 thin slices off the top of each celeriac, reserving the majority of the celeriac for later.

In a large pot, heat the oil to 300°F (150°C), using a thermometer to be accurate. Fry the shaved celeriac until it doesn't bubble in the oil and is golden all over, agitating it in the oil throughout to ensure an even cook. Using a skimmer, remove the celeriac bark and place it on a paper towel to drain. Sprinkle with salt or hemlock salt. Reserve the oil for later.

MAKE THE FONDANT: Cut each of the remaining celeriac pieces into three thick slices roughly 1 inch (2.5 cm) thick. Use a ring cutter to cut six perfect and equal-size circles from the celeriac slices. Reserve the trim for later.

In a wide pan that will snugly hold all six celeriac pucks, heat the 1 cup (230 g) butter until foaming. Add the celeriac pucks and cook, with the butter continuing to foam, until each puck is well golden on one side. Flip the celeriac and add the sprig of thyme, the garlic, and some salt. Continue to cook until the celeriac is tender, then finish with the lemon juice and leave to cool in the butter.

Recipe continues ▶

⅓ cup (35 g) cynamoka berries

Salt and cracked black pepper

¼ cup (60 g) butter

1 lb (450 g) chanterelle mushrooms, cleaned and cut into
bite-size pieces

Cynamoka berry gel (recipe
follows) (optional)

⅓ cup (80 mL) hemlock oil
(page 261)

Elk crackers (recipe follows)
(optional)

Pickled hemlock tips (page 264)
(optional)

Wild bitter cress

SERVES 6

MAKE THE PURÉE: Chop the celeriac trim into small pieces, then place in a small pot with the milk, making sure the milk covers the celeriac. (Add more if necessary.) Add a pinch of salt and simmer over medium heat until the celeriac is soft enough to purée. Drain the milk from the celeriac and blend on high speed until smooth. Reserve in a warm place until ready to use.

TO ASSEMBLE: If they are not already warm, heat the celeriac purée, fondant, and elk jus, then add the cynamoka berries to the jus.

Season the elk portions with salt and pepper. Place a sauté pan or skillet big enough to hold all the elk pieces over high heat and add the butter. When the butter is hot, place the elk in the pan and sear, flipping once, until medium-rare. Remove from the pan and allow it to rest.

Place the chanterelles in the pan and cook until tender, then season with salt and pepper.

On six plates, arrange small dots of cynamoka berry gel (if using) and place one large dollop of celeriac purée right in the middle. Place a celeriac fondant on top of the purée.

Slice the roasted and rested elk and arrange on top of the fondant. Top the elk with the chanterelles, letting them spill naturally off of the meat.

Drizzle the plates with the hemlock oil and elk jus, making sure to scoop the berries onto the plates. Arrange crackers (if using) on each plate so that they look like a pile of leaves hiding the elk. Finish with pickled hemlock tips (if using) and wild bitter cress for colour.

INN-STYLE

When Executive Chef Barr makes this dish, he's trying to recreate the essence of the forest floor with multiple components that evoke fallen leaves, scattered needles, the berries that peek from the foliage, and the mushrooms that grow amid the tree roots. Home cooks may find this an overwhelming project; for one thing, some of the ingredients are hard to come by outside the Tofino area. Luckily, the seared elk and its jus make an irresistible centrepiece to a meal with whatever sides you wish to prepare. However, those who want to make this extraordinarily beautiful dish authentically Inn-style will want to add a few dabs of cynamoka berry gel on the plate and top the whole dish with a few elk crackers (both recipes below).

Cynamoka Berry Gel

In a pan set over medium-high heat, combine all the ingredients and bring to a boil for 10 seconds, stirring regularly. Transfer to a small container and chill in the fridge until set hard. Dice the gel and blend until smooth.

7 oz (200 g) cynamoka berries, currants, or huckleberries, picked clean

⅜ cup (90 mL) water

1 Tbsp (15 mL) red wine vinegar

1 Tbsp (15 mL) honey

1 tsp (2 g) agar powder (a vegan gelatin substitute)

MAKES ABOUT ½ CUP (125 ML) GEL

Elk Crackers

Mince the elk meat and place in a blender with the tapioca flour and water. Season with salt and pepper and blend until smooth. Pass through a strainer and spread evenly on a silicone liner to a thickness of 1/16 inch (2 mm). Note that the silicone liner will need to fit into a steamer.

Transfer the silicone liner to a small baking sheet and wrap tightly in plastic wrap, making sure that the plastic wrap doesn't touch the surface of the elk paste. Prepare a steamer that will fit the tray and steam for 15 minutes or until the paste is cooked and the cracker base forms.

Unwrap the cracker base and leave uncovered at room temperature for 48 hours until it is completely dry.

When you're ready to prepare the crackers, heat the oil in a large pot to 350°F (180°C). Break the cracker base into small pieces, then place into the hot oil for just a few seconds. The crackers should puff quickly and turn golden brown. Using a skimmer, remove from the oil, drain on paper towels, and season with salt and porcini powder.

3 oz (85 g) elk meat, sinew removed

⅔ cup (80 g) tapioca flour

⅔ cup (160 mL) water

Salt and cracked black pepper to taste

Canola oil for frying

1 Tbsp (6 g) porcini mushroom powder

SERVES 6

Gloriously big, rich, meaty scallops have a delicate flavour that partners beautifully with pork belly. Executive Chef Barr's dish combining the two is a masterpiece of textures and a delightful marriage of land and sea on one plate.

CRISPY PORK BELLY and SCALLOPS

PORK BELLY

3 cloves garlic, peeled

¼ cup (55 g) packed brown sugar

¼ cup (35 g) salt, plus additional
   as needed

1 sprig thyme

2 lb (900 g) pork belly, skin on

2 onions

1-inch (2.5 cm) piece of ginger,
   peeled

½ cup (125 mL) apple cider
   vinegar

2 cups (500 mL) apple juice

SUNCHOKE PURÉE

1½ lb (675 g) sunchokes, unpeeled

Salt to taste

2 Tbsp (30 g) butter

2 cups (500 mL) milk

Cracked black pepper to taste

ASSEMBLY

1 lb (450 g) scallops

Salt

1¼ cups (310 mL) +1 Tbsp (15 mL)
   canola oil

Lemon juice

1 bunch kale, torn into bite-size
   pieces

30 red grapes

SERVES 6

MAKE THE PORK BELLY: Crush one clove of garlic and, in a bowl, combine it with the brown sugar, salt, and thyme. Rub the mixture between your hands to release the aromas, then pat the mixture all over the flesh side of the pork belly. Place in a dish, skin side up, and leave uncovered in the fridge overnight to cure.

Preheat the oven to 400°F (200°C). Slice the onions, remaining garlic, and ginger and arrange on the bottom of a small roasting pan. Wash the cure off the pork belly and pat dry. Place on top of the sliced vegetables, skin side up, and add the vinegar and apple juice to the pan. Sprinkle some salt over the skin of the pork belly, then tightly wrap the whole roasting pan in aluminum foil. Place in the oven and steam-roast for 30 minutes.

Remove the pork belly from the oven and take off the foil. At this point the skin should be soft and slightly translucent. Score the skin with a sharp knife in a crisscross pattern about 1 inch (2.5 cm) apart. Return to the oven for another 30 minutes, then turn the oven down to 275°F (135°C) and cook until the skin is deep gold and hard, at least two hours, possibly more. (If you have a convection oven, the fan will help with this process considerably; just remember to reduce the heat of your oven to 250°F/120°C to compensate for the fan.)

Remove the pork belly from the oven and cool to room temperature, reserving any juices in the pan for later. Place the belly between two small baking sheets and apply some weight to the top to flatten it. Place the whole assembly in the refrigerator overnight.

The next day, cut the belly into six even portions and set aside until ready to serve.

Recipe continues ▶

MAKE THE SUNCHOKE PURÉE: Preheat the oven to 300°F (150°C). Season 1 lb (450 g) of the sunchokes with salt and wrap in an aluminum-foil pouch so that they lie flat. Bake for 45 minutes or until the sunchokes are very soft. Cool to room temperature, then cut them in half.

Chop the remaining ½ lb (225 g) sunchokes into small pieces. In a wide pot, heat the butter until brown and foaming. Add the sunchokes and roast until lightly golden, about 20 minutes. Add the milk and cook until the sunchokes are soft, another 10 to 15 minutes. In a blender or food processor, blend until smooth. Season with salt and pepper and reserve in a warm place.

TO ASSEMBLE: When you're ready to assemble the dish, preheat the oven to 350°F (180°C).

Season the scallops with salt and leave to dry on a paper towel.

In a wide frying pan, heat a couple of tablespoons (about 30 mL) of the canola oil over medium heat. Once the oil is hot, sprinkle a touch of salt evenly in the pan, then add the pieces of pork belly, skin side down, and place uncovered in the oven.

In another frying pan, heat another couple of tablespoons (about 30 mL) of the canola oil over medium heat and cook the sunchokes, cut side down, until well caramelized, about 10 minutes. Remove them from the oil and season with salt.

Wipe out the sunchoke pan, add another splash of canola oil, and heat over high heat until the oil ripples. Sear the scallops on one side until well golden (this will take only a couple of minutes), then flip them and remove them from the heat. After a few seconds, remove the scallops from the pan and season them with lemon juice to taste.

Remove the pork belly from the oven. By now the skin should be well puffed and crispy. If it is still a bit rubbery, cook on the stovetop until the skin has finished puffing. Drain the oil from the pan and turn the belly pieces over. If you have any remaining juice from roasting the belly earlier, add it to the pan.

On six plates, swirl some of the sunchoke purée. Arrange the scallops, sunchokes, and pork belly attractively on the plate. In a high-heat pan, add a tablespoon (15 mL) of canola oil then quickly wilt the kale and grapes, then use them to garnish the plates.

INN-STYLE

At the Inn, Chef Barr adds touches of bright, crisp acidity to balance out the unctuousness of the pork, scallops, and creamy sunchokes. He adds a dollop of raisin purée to the swirls of sunchoke purée and a spoonful of verjus mustard (page 264) to the pork. Verjus is a tart, fragrant condiment halfway between grape juice and vinegar, and it makes a delicious addition to many dressings and sauces.

Inside Henry Nolla's carving shed

This fragrant dish from Chef Springett can easily go casual or formal. Serve it simply with grilled vegetables (as pictured opposite), or add the orange sauce, orange confit and duck confit potatoes (pages 170 to 171) for a truly special dish. Either way the duck is infused with irresistable layers of spice and citrus flavour.

Cinnamon-Scented DUCK BREAST

DUCK

2 Tbsp (10 g) ground cinnamon

2 to 4 sprigs thyme, leaves only

Finely grated zest of 1 orange

Cracked black pepper to taste

4 juniper berries, finely ground

4 duck breasts, sinew and tender removed, fat scored

Sea salt to taste

2 Tbsp (30 mL) grapeseed oil, or as needed

2 cloves garlic, skin on

2 sprigs thyme

2 Tbsp (30 g) butter

TO SERVE

Orange sauce (page 170) (optional)

Orange segment confit (page 170) (optional)

Duck confit potato press (page 171) (optional)

SERVES 4

MARINATE THE DUCK: In a small bowl, mix together the cinnamon, thyme, orange zest, pepper, and ground junipers. Rub all over the flesh side of the duck breasts. Place in the refrigerator and chill overnight; to get a crispier skin, leave the duck uncovered.

MAKE THE DUCK: Preheat a gas or charcoal grill to 350°F (180°C) or preheat the oven to 350°F (180°C).

Season the duck with sea salt. Heat an ovenproof sauté pan to medium-high heat, add the oil, and place the duck breasts, fat side down, in the pan. Lower the heat to medium-low and cook until the fat turns golden brown. As the fat renders, remove it from the pan with a spoon and reserve to use for another purpose later.

If you are using the barbecue, place the seared duck skin side up on the grill (or a preheated grill pan, if you prefer) over indirect heat. Close the lid and roast for about 5 minutes to medium rare, or until it reaches your preferred doneness. Flip the duck breast and finish it skin side down over direct heat for another minute or two, until the skin is crispy and has attractive grill marks. Allow it to rest for 8 to 10 minutes before serving—you can grill some orange slices, carrots, broccolini, or other vegetables while you wait.

If you are using the oven, leave the duck in the pan, but turn the breasts over to quickly sear the flesh, then flip back onto the fatty side, place the pan in the oven, and roast until the duck has reached your preferred doneness—it will take only about 5 minutes to reach medium-rare.

Remove from the oven and add the garlic cloves, thyme sprigs, and butter to the pan, allowing everything to rest for 8 to 10 minutes in the pan before slicing the duck.

Divide the duck breasts between four plates. Serve with grilled vegetables and orange slices or, for a more formal presentation, drizzle with orange sauce and serve with orange segment confit and duck confit potato press.

Recipe continues ▶

ORANGE SEGMENT CONFIT

5 large oranges

1¼ cups (250 g) sugar

2 cups (500 mL) water

1 sprig thyme

Finely grated zest of 1 lemon

4 pods green cardamom, crushed

1 bay leaf

5 turns cracked black pepper, or
    to taste

Pinch of salt

**MAKES ABOUT 2 CUPS
(500 ML)**

Cut the oranges into segments, remove the peels and membrane, and reserve any juice. Place into a non-reactive, heatproof bowl and set aside.

In a stainless steel pot, place all the remaining ingredients and simmer for 15 minutes. Let cool for 10 minutes, then pour over the orange segments and their juice. Let the confit sit at room temperature for 30 minutes, then store in the fridge until ready to use.

ORANGE SAUCE

SAUCE

4 Tbsp (60 mL) apple cider
    vinegar

4 Tbsp (50 g) sugar

2 bay leaves

2 juniper berries, crushed

1 cup (250 mL) orange juice

2 cups (500 mL) duck stock
    (page 272)

Salt and cracked black pepper

2 Tbsp (30 g) cold butter

**MAKES ABOUT 1 CUP
(250 ML)**

PREPARE THE SAUCE: In a small saucepan, combine the vinegar, sugar, bay leaves, and crushed junipers and cook over medium heat until reduced by three-quarters (this should take 10 to 15 minutes). Add the orange juice and reduce by half (another 30 minutes or so), then add the duck stock and reduce until it is thick enough to coat the back of a spoon and not run off. This will take about another 30 minutes.

Just before serving, season with salt and pepper, then whisk in the cold butter.

In this side dish by Chef Springett, layers of tender potatoes are interspersed with rich duck confit, a perfect partner for his cinnamon-scented duck breast (page 168) or any other roast meat dish. Find directions for making rendered duck fat, duck stock, and confit duck legs on pages 272 to 273.

DUCK CONFIT POTATO PRESS

Preheat the oven to 350°F (180°C).

Peel the potatoes and slice them thinly and evenly; do not rinse. Dress the potatoes with duck fat, salt, pepper, thyme leaves, and lemon zest.

Line a rimmed baking sheet with parchment paper, then layer the potatoes on the sheet, making sure they overlap. Cover the potatoes with another sheet of parchment, then aluminum foil, and bake until cooked, about 30 minutes. Remove from the oven and remove the foil, but leave the parchment on. Allow to cool to room temperature, then cover with another baking sheet, press together, and set in the fridge until cool, about 2 hours.

Warm the confit duck legs; if they seem dry, add a little duck fat and/or stock.

Cut the potato sheet into three equal-size rectangles. Divide the confit meat in half and press evenly on top of two of the potato rectangles. Place one of these triangles on top of the other, then top with the sheet that has no confit on top.

Once assembled, wrap the edges with aluminum foil for support, cover with parchment, and press again for a few hours or overnight before cutting into portions.

To serve, reheat in a 250°F (120°C) oven for about 30 minutes or until heated through.

3 lb (1.5 kg) Yukon gold potatoes

½ cup (125 mL) duck fat, or as needed, melted (page 272)

Salt and cracked black pepper to taste

Thyme leaves, no stems, to taste

Finely grated zest of 2 lemons, no pith

4 confit duck legs, skin and bones removed, shredded (page 273)

SERVES 4 TO 6

Chef Springett's very first menu at the Inn featured this decadent terrine of creamy foie gras parfait and tender smoked salmon. It became one of his all-time favourites—and the favourite of many guests, too. He served it in a luxurious presentation with a tower of potato salad, local sturgeon caviar, and classic caviar garnishes, but even served on its own it is perfectly extraordinary.

FOIE GRAS and SMOKED SALMON TERRINE

MARINADE

½ tsp (2 g) salt

½ tsp (2 g) sugar

½ tsp (1 g) cayenne pepper

6 sprigs thyme

Zest of 1 lemon, no pith, julienned

2 Tbsp (30 mL) brandy

1 lobe grade A foie gras, 1 lb
    (450 g)

TERRINE

1 cup (225 g) mascarpone cheese,
    room temperature

Finely grated zest of 1 lemon

Salt and cayenne pepper to taste

⅜ cup (90 mL) cream

25 slices lean, cold-smoked
    salmon, thinly sliced into
    terrine-size sheets

MAKES 1 TERRINE

MARINATE THE FOIE GRAS: Mix the salt, sugar, cayenne, thyme, lemon zest, and brandy together. Slice the foie into 1-inch (2.5 cm) thick slices. Pat the marinade over all sides of the foie, place in a resealable bag (removing the air), and rest in the refrigerator overnight.

MAKE THE TERRINE: Line a terrine mould with plastic wrap, making sure a fair amount of the plastic wrap hangs over the edge of the dish to aid in removing the terrine later.

Heat a pan of water to 185°F (85°C). Place the bag containing the foie into the simmering water and heat until half the fat has been rendered and, when you press it between your fingers, it does not have any firm spots like cold butter. Remove the foie from the bag and pass through a sieve into a bowl that has been placed on ice, removing any veins as well as the marinade.

Whisk the melted foie in the cold bowl until it begins to re-emulsify but is not solid—it should be spreadable, like room-temperature butter. Remove the bowl from the ice.

Using a spatula, fold the mascarpone and lemon zest into the bowl of foie, then season with salt and cayenne. Beat the cream until it forms soft peaks, then fold that into the foie mixture by hand. Place into a piping bag with a wide tip.

Shingle a layer of smoked salmon on the bottom of the terrine mould, then pipe a ½-inch (1 cm) layer of mousse on top. Shingle another layer of salmon on top of the mousse, and repeat until you reach the top of the terrine but don't go over the edge—the final layer should be of smoked salmon.

Fold the plastic wrap over the top of the terrine, making sure it is fully sealed and there are no creases in it. Place a flat board over the terrine and a moderately heavy weight to press it overnight.

Keep the terrine chilled until you are ready to serve. Remove from the mould, cut into ten slices (a hot bevelled knife will make this easier), and serve.

Recipe continues ▶

INN-STYLE

At the Inn, Chef Springett served this luxurious terrine alongside a tower of fingerling potato salad and a garnish of Northern Divine caviar and traditional accoutrements. Northern Divine is a small company on British Columbia's Sunshine Coast that produces high-quality, sustainable sturgeon caviar beloved by local chefs. If you wish to make this dish Inn-style, this is how to do it.

1 recipe Fingerling Potato Salad
  (page 191)
1 foie gras and smoked salmon
  terrine (recipe above)

GARNISHES

10 pieces russet potato gaufrette
  (thinly sliced potatoes fried
  until crispy)
10 tufts frisée lettuce, refreshed
  in ice water
5 hard-boiled egg whites, finely
  grated
5 hard-boiled egg yolks, finely
  grated
Northern Divine caviar
⅜ cup (18 g) finely chopped
  chives
Chive flowers

MAKES 10 SERVINGS

Divide the potato salad between ten plates, then form into a tall, round tower placed toward the back of the plate at 12 o'clock.

With a hot bevelled knife, slice the terrine into ¼-inch (6 mm) thick slices. Place a terrine slice in front of the potato salad on each plate. Place a gaufrette potato on top of each tower and a tuft of frisée on top of each gaufrette.

In a circle around the terrine, arrange the other garnishes—egg white, egg yolk, and caviar. Lightly dress the egg and caviar with some of the lemon dressing from the potato salad. Garnish with chives and chive flowers.

"This smoked-meat recipe is dead simple and is such a joy to cook," says Chef Labossiere. It takes a week to brine, and then most of a day to smoke the brisket, but there is actually very little work involved. The end result is tender, smoky, flavourful meat, ideal on its own or tucked inside a sandwich.

SMOKED BRISKET

BRINE THE BRISKET: In a large bowl or container, combine the brine ingredients and mix well until everything is dissolved. Using a brining needle, inject 1 cup (250 mL) of the brine solution into the brisket. Pour the remaining brine into a large roasting pan, then place the injected brisket into the brine. Cover and refrigerate for 7 days, flipping the brisket every 2 days.

MAKE THE RUB: In a skillet over medium heat, toast all the spices separately. Allow to cool, then grind them fine and mix together. Combine with the salt.

Prepare a smoker: Light the charcoal and add chunks of soaked fruitwood such as apple and/or cherry. Bring the chamber to a heat of around 210°F (100°C).

Remove the brisket from the brine and lightly pat it with a towel, but do not dry completely, as the rub will stick better if the brisket is still slightly moist. Completely coat the brisket in the rub.

Place the brisket in the smoker and smoke for 10 hours. Resist the urge to peek inside except when replenishing the charcoal; you want to maintain as consistent a heat of 210°F (100°C) as possible.

Remove the brisket and serve warm or cool. This is delicious in sandwiches, and the excess freezes well.

If you don't have a smoker, this recipe makes for great pastrami-style beef: After it has brined for a week, place the brisket in a covered roasting pan and bake in a convection oven at 250°F (120°C) for 6 to 8 hours or until tender.

12 lb (5.5 kg) fresh beef brisket, trimmed to a uniform fat cap

BRINE
16 cups (4 L) water
1 cup (220 g) packed brown sugar
½ cup (70 g) salt
5 tsp (25 g) curing salt (see note)
6 bay leaves
5 tsp (15 g) black peppercorns, toasted
5 tsp (10 g) yellow mustard seeds

RUB
2 Tbsp (10 g) coriander seeds
7 Tbsp (65 g) black peppercorns
1½ Tbsp (10 g) chili flakes
1½ Tbsp (10 g) fennel seeds
¼ cup (35 g) salt

SERVES A CROWD

A NOTE ABOUT CURING SALT

Curing salt, also known as F.S. Cure, Prague Powder, or pink salt, is available in specialty gourmet or butcher-supply stores. It comprises about 95 percent sodium chloride and 5 percent sodium nitrite—the nitrite ensures a safer, more consistent cure. Please note, though, that this salt is not edible and should never be used as a seasoning salt.

Venison adds a delicate depth to Chef Butters's non-traditional version of the classic Italian appetizer. But if venison is unavailable, beef, veal, or bison may be substituted, as long as the meat is of the highest quality and as sinew-free as possible. He suggests pairing it with Haywire Winery's soft, plush 2014 Gamay Noir.

VENISON CARPACCIO

VENISON

1 tsp (2 g) cracked black pepper

1 tsp (2 g) finely chopped
   rosemary

1 Tbsp (4 g) finely chopped thyme
   leaves

1 Tbsp (4 g) finely chopped
   flat-leaf parsley

8 to 10 oz (225 to 280 g) piece
   boneless venison, preferably
   Denver leg, loin, or tenderloin

1 Tbsp (15 mL) grapeseed oil

MUSTARD DRESSING

1 Tbsp (15 mL) Dijon mustard

2 Tbsp (30 mL) white wine
   vinegar

2 Tbsp (30 mL) grapeseed oil

1 Tbsp (3 g) finely chopped chives

1 shallot, finely chopped

2 cloves garlic, finely chopped

1 Tbsp (15 mL) honey

ASSEMBLY

1 apple, cored and as thinly sliced
   as possible (optional)

Watercress

¼ cup (30 g) chopped walnuts,
   toasted

Coarse sea salt

Baguette slices, grilled, 3 to 4
   slices per person

SERVES 4 TO 6

PREPARE THE VENISON: Mix together the pepper, rosemary, thyme, and parsley and rub all over the venison.

Heat a cast-iron skillet until quite hot. Add the venison and drizzle the oil overtop. Be careful to avoid any splatters, as the pan should be very hot. Brown the venison on all sides, but do not cook. You want a nice crust on the entire outside of the meat while leaving the centre raw.

Remove from the pan and let cool to room temperature. Wrap in plastic wrap into a very tight cylinder. Wrap again in a thin layer of aluminum foil to make the cylinder even tighter. Put in the freezer until frozen.

MAKE THE MUSTARD DRESSING: In a small non-reactive bowl, combine all ingredients. Keep refrigerated until ready to use.

TO ASSEMBLE: Remove the venison from the freezer for about 20 minutes to slightly temper before slicing. Slice the venison as thinly as possible. Immediately place the slices onto individual plates—it will thaw very quickly, making it difficult to handle.

Arrange the apple slices over the carpaccio, drizzle with mustard dressing, and generously garnish with fresh watercress and walnuts. Sprinkle with coarse sea salt and serve with grilled baguette slices.

Executive Chef Barr has discovered that Vancouver Island produces plump, flavourful chickens, best prepared as simply as possible to preserve their flavour and texture. Here he uses a traditional culinary technique—pan-frying and basting with butter, thyme, and garlic—then layers on glorious textures and flavours.

Vancouver Island CHICKEN with SUNFLOWER SEED RISOTTO

CHICKEN

½ cup (70 g) salt, plus more for
   pan-frying
½ cup (100 g) sugar
8 cups (2 L) water
4 chicken breasts, skin on
⅓ cup (80 mL) canola oil, or as
   needed
1 clove garlic
1 sprig thyme
2 Tbsp (30 g) butter

**SUNFLOWER SEED
RISOTTO**

2 cups (285 g) unsalted sunflower
   seeds
1 tsp (5 g) baking soda
1 tsp (3 g) salt, plus additional for
   seasoning
4 cups (1 L) vegetable stock, plus
   additional for reheating
Pesto (page 274)
Butter, if needed
Parmesan cheese, grated

CARROTS

16 baby carrots, including tops
2 cups (500 mL) vegetable stock
Salt to taste
1 Tbsp (15 g) butter
Juice of 1 lemon

Smoked almond cream (page 275)
   (optional)

SERVES 4

THE DAY BEFORE SERVING THIS DISH, BRINE THE CHICKEN: In a pot, combine the salt, sugar, and water and bring to a boil. Cool in the refrigerator, then add the chicken breasts, return to the fridge, and brine for 6 hours. Remove the chicken from the brine, rinse, and pat dry. Leave in the fridge overnight, skin side up and uncovered.

START THE SUNFLOWER SEED RISOTTO: In a pot, combine the sunflower seeds, baking soda, salt, and vegetable stock and simmer for 30 minutes. Drain the liquid and rinse the sunflower seeds briefly under running water. Reserve in the fridge until needed.

PREPARE THE CHICKEN: Over high heat, heat a pan big enough for the chicken breasts. Once the pan is hot, add the canola oil and spread a pinch of salt evenly in the pan. Place the chicken breasts in the pan skin side down. Roast over medium heat until the skin is golden and crispy. Flip the chicken over and pour off the oil. Add the garlic, thyme, and butter, letting it brown, and continue to cook over low heat, basting the chicken the whole time. Cook like this for 5 minutes, then turn off the heat, leave the pan uncovered and continue to baste until the chicken is cooked through, about 20 minutes in total.

MAKE THE CARROTS: Scrub the baby carrots and trim their tops, leaving ½ inch (1 cm) of green on the carrots. Save the tops for garnish. In a wide pan, combine the carrots with the vegetable stock and salt to taste. Cook over high heat until the carrots are just tender, about 5 minutes, then remove them from the pan. Reduce the stock to a glaze, add the butter and lemon juice, then return the carrots to the pan.

FINISH THE SUNFLOWER SEED RISOTTO: In a pan, heat the sunflower seeds and a splash of stock, then add some pesto to your liking. Adjust consistency with butter, more stock, and/or Parmesan cheese.

TO ASSEMBLE: If you like, place a few scoops of smoked almond purée on four plates. Spoon sunflower seed risotto onto each plate, then place a chicken breast in the centre of each. Add the carrots and a bit more pesto, and garnish with carrot-top fronds.

Executive Chef Barr considers this his most memorable dish. "I find carrots provide an unexpected way to deliver a memorable experience, as they are so plain and unexciting to the common diner," he says. "In this dish they become a great vehicle for nostalgia, as everybody has a fond memory of their mom's spaghetti. Of course, this dish allows our vegetarian diners to take a stroll down memory lane as well."

CARROT BOLOGNAISE with RUTABAGA SPAGHETTI

Scrub the purple carrots, quarter them lengthwise, and pass them through a grinder set to the coarsest setting or grate them on the large holes of a box grater. (Unless they are quite dirty, you don't need to peel the carrots.)

Heat a large saucepan until quite hot. Add ½ cup (115 g) butter and cook until foaming and just starting to brown. Add half the sliced garlic and cook until it starts to caramelize. Add the ground carrots and cook until most of the liquid is evaporated and the carrots shrink by about two-thirds. This should take about 30 to 45 minutes. Remove from the heat, scrape into a bowl, and set aside.

Clean the original pot and return to medium heat. Add the remaining ½ cup (115 g) butter to the pot and heat until foamy, then add the onions, star anise, and pepper. Cook over medium heat until well caramelized.

Add the red wine and red wine vinegar and continue cooking until the liquid is reduced by half, about 20 minutes. Add the tomatoes, bay leaves, and two sprigs of thyme. Cook until reduced to a thick consistency, about 20 minutes, then add the cooked ground carrots. Set aside.

In a large saucepan over medium heat, heat the olive oil, then add the leeks, diced orange carrots, celery, the remaining garlic, two more sprigs of thyme, the oregano, and the chili flakes. Cook until the vegetables are soft. Add the carrot mixture. Combine all ingredients into one pot and check the seasoning. Serve over pasta or the rutabaga spaghetti that follows.

Recipe continues ▶

4 lb (1.8 kg) purple carrots

1 cup (230 g) butter

4 cloves garlic, sliced

2 onions, sliced

1 pod star anise

½ tsp (1 g) cracked black pepper

750 mL bottle red wine

¼ cup (60 mL) red wine vinegar

1 (28 oz/794 g) can crushed
   tomatoes

2 bay leaves

4 sprigs thyme

¼ cup (60 mL) olive oil

1 leek, white part only, diced small

½ large orange carrot, diced small

1 stick celery, diced small

2 sprigs oregano, leaves only,
   sliced into chiffonade

½ tsp (1 g) chili flakes

**MAKES ABOUT 6 CUPS
(1.5 L)**

Rutabaga Spaghetti

3 large rutabagas, peeled

2 Tbsp (18 g) salt, plus additional for seasoning

1 cup (250 mL) water, plus additional for rinsing the rutabagas

¼ cup (60 mL) olive oil

Carrot bolognaise (page 181)

3 sprigs oregano, leaves only, chopped

2 sprigs flat-leaf parsley, leaves only, chopped

Cracked black pepper

Parmesan cheese, grated

SERVES 6

It looks like pasta, but in fact is the humble rutabaga, a cabbage-turnip hybrid that is low in calories but high in fibre, vitamin C, potassium, and other nutrients. Executive Chef Barr likes to serve this as a dish that is both whimsical and nutritious, as well as satisfying to vegetarian guests, especially when topped with his carrot bolognaise (page 181).

Using a spiralizer, turn the rutabaga into long noodles. Toss in the 2 Tbsp (18 g) salt and let stand for 1 hour.

Submerge in water to rinse off the extra salt. You may need to change the water several times to remove all of the salt. The rutabaga noodles should be pliable yet firm.

In a large pot, heat 1 cup (250 mL) water and the olive oil, then add the rutabaga noodles. Heat and cook them until they are just al dente.

In a separate pan, heat the carrot bolognaise. Stir in the chopped oregano and parsley and season with salt and pepper.

Using a carving fork, turn six nice spiral mounds of noodles and place in the centre of six bowls. Top with the carrot bolognaise and finish with as much Parmesan cheese as you enjoy.

Our chefs have always taken care to provide delicious options for vegetarians, including Chef Butters's beautiful root-vegetable torte. This makes a great vegetarian main course, or even a side dish for meat lovers. Those avoiding dairy can skip the cheese and replace the cream with chicken or vegetable stock.

ROOT-VEGETABLE TORTE

VEGETABLES

2 large carrots

2 large red or gold beets

1 medium rutabaga

2 medium white turnips

6 sunchokes (optional)

1 small celeriac

2 medium parsnips

2 russet potatoes

FILLING

3 cloves garlic, finely chopped

3 large shallots, very thinly sliced

½ cup (50 g) grated Parmesan or your choice of cheese

1 cup (250 mL) cream

¼ cup (15 g) chopped herbs, such as flat-leaf parsley, thyme, and/or tarragon

Sea salt

Cracked black pepper

TOPPING

3 oz (85 g) mild goat cheese or ricotta

SERVES 4 TO 6

PREPARE THE VEGETABLES: Preheat the oven to 400°F (200°C). Spray a deep 8-inch (20 cm) square ovenproof casserole dish with non-stick spray or line the entire dish with parchment paper. (Use the parchment paper, with excess hanging over the sides, if you want to remove the torte from the pan to pre-slice.)

Using a mandoline if you have one, peel and slice all the vegetables as thinly as possible. Keep each type of vegetable separate from the others.

MAKE THE FILLING: Mix together the ingredients for the filling and set aside.

ASSEMBLE THE TORTE: Place a layer of one of the vegetables in the bottom of the dish; sprinkle some of the filling on top. Continue to alternate vegetables and filling until the casserole dish is full. Try alternating different colours of vegetables for the greatest effect.

Crumble the goat cheese or ricotta over the top layer. Put the casserole dish on a baking sheet, cover very loosely with aluminum foil or parchment paper, and place in the oven.

Bake for about 50 to 60 minutes or until the centre of the casserole feels tender when a fork is inserted. Remove from the oven and let stand for a few minutes before serving. This can be served directly from the pan or removed and sliced for a more dramatic presentation.

Executive Chef Barr takes the humble cauliflower and transforms it into a luxurious dish rich with the earthy flavours of truffles. He recommends black truffles from France's Périgord region, but with the emerging commercial production of truffles on Vancouver Island, he may start looking closer to home. Best of all, this is a decadent dish that will appeal to carnivores and vegetarians alike.

TRUFFLED CAULIFLOWER "RISOTTO"

2 small heads cauliflower

2 cups (500 mL) milk

3 shallots, finely chopped

2 cups (500 mL) white wine

½ cup (125 mL) vegetable stock

3 Tbsp (45 mL) truffle paste

1 Tbsp (15 mL) truffle oil

1 bunch flat-leaf parsley, sliced
into chiffonade

1 bunch chives, chopped

¼ cup (60 g) butter

2 oz (60 g) Alpindon cheese
(a firm cow's milk cheese from
Kootenay Alpine Cheese Co.,
similar to French Beaufort
d'Alpage), or to taste

½ oz (15 g) fresh truffles,
preferably Périgord

1 bunch chervil, leaves only

2 cured egg yolks (page 273)
(optional)

SERVES 6

Make the cauliflower "rice": Remove and discard any leaves from the cauliflower. Use a knife to remove all of the florets. Grind all of the florets in a food processor so they resemble small grains of rice. Set aside.

Thinly slice the remaining cauliflower stems and place in a wide pot with the milk. Simmer until the cauliflower is tender, then drain off the milk and purée in a blender or food processor.

Place the shallots in a small pot with the white wine and cook down until almost dry.

Place the cauliflower "rice" in a wide pan with the white-wine shallots and vegetable stock and cook until almost dry. Do not overcook; it should still have some texture.

Stir in some of the cauliflower purée and the truffle paste, truffle oil, parsley, chives, and butter and mix vigorously to emulsify. Grate in half of the cheese and mix again. At this point the risotto should be rich and creamy and resemble a traditional risotto.

Distribute between six bowls and tap the bottom of each bowl to flatten the risotto. Finish each dish with additional grated cheese, shaved truffle (use a mandoline or a truffle shaver), chervil, and optional grated cured egg yolk.

In spring and fall, the forests around the Inn are filled with edible wild mushrooms: delicate chanterelles, meaty pine mushrooms, smoky morels. Foragers bring them to the Inn's chefs, who then transform them into earthy dishes like this simple stuffed pasta by Chef Ly. Of course, regular button mushrooms will also work.

MUSHROOM TORTELLINI with CHIVE OIL

PASTA DOUGH
2¾ cups (345 g) flour, plus
    additional for rolling
⅞ cup (145 g) semolina flour
2 eggs
1 egg yolk
Pinch of salt
2 tsp (10 mL) olive oil

CHIVE OIL
1 small bunch chives
½ cup (125 mL) olive oil

MUSHROOM FILLING
1 lb (450 g) button or mixed
    mushrooms, roughly chopped
1 shallot, finely diced
1 clove garlic, finely chopped
1 sprig thyme, leaves only
¼ cup (60 mL) sherry
2 tsp (10 mL) whipping cream

SERVES 2

PREPARE THE PASTA: In a stand mixer fitted with a dough hook, combine all the ingredients and mix for approximately 10 minutes or until smooth and slightly springy to the touch. Form it into a ball and allow it to rest for about 30 minutes.

Using a pasta roller, roll out the pasta dough into thin sheets. Divide the dough into three smaller portions, and feed the first through the pasta machine at its widest setting. Turn the setting a notch narrower and feed the sheet through again, repeating until the sheet is quite thin, but not so thin it will tear. You may need to dust the dough generously with flour so it doesn't stick to the rollers. Repeat with the remaining portions of pasta dough. Allow the pasta sheets to rest in the fridge for 30 minutes.

Using a round 3-inch (8 cm) cookie cutter, punch out 16 circles from the pasta sheet. Cover the pasta with a damp towel until ready to use.

Meanwhile, make the chive oil: In a blender, combine the chives and oil and blend for about 3 minutes. Strain the oil through a fine-mesh strainer.

MAKE THE MUSHROOM FILLING: In a medium saucepan, sweat the mushrooms for about 2 minutes, then add the shallots, garlic, and thyme and continue cooking for about 3 more minutes. Add the sherry and reduce the liquid until dry, then add the cream and cook for about 1 minute. Remove from the heat and allow to cool.

When the mushroom mixture has cooled, place one small dollop of the mixture in the centre of each pasta circle. Fold the pasta in half over the mixture, forming a half-moon shape. Then fold the two ends together and press tightly to form the tortellini. Whisk a little flour and water together to create a paste and use it to seal the tortellini. Repeat the steps until you have 16 tortellini.

Bring a large pot of salted water to a boil, then carefully drop the tortellini into the water and cook for 3 minutes. They should float to the top when they are ready. With a skimmer, remove the tortellini from the water, divide between two plates, and drizzle with chive oil.

*Adding truffles to humble gnocchi transforms them into decadent little bites
with a wonderfully earthy flavour. Chef Labossiere's recipe keeps the toppings
simple—just butter, oil, parsley, and cheese—to allow the truffly flavours to
really shine.*

BLACK-TRUFFLE GNOCCHI

1 tsp (5 g) fine sea salt, plus more
    for pan

4 large Yukon gold potatoes

4 cups (500 g) flour, sifted
    (approximately)

4 egg yolks (approximately)

½ cup (70 g) salt

1 to 2 Tbsp (15 to 30 g) black-
    truffle tapenade, purée, or
    paste, or chopped black truffles

1 Tbsp (15 g) softened butter

1 Tbsp (15 mL) good-quality olive
    oil

1 Tbsp (4 g) chopped flat-leaf
    parsley

½ cup (50 g) grated pecorino
    romano cheese, or to taste

SERVES 4 TO 6

Preheat the oven to 375°F (190°C). Line a small baking pan with salt to
create a bed.

Using a knife or fork, generously poke the unpeeled potatoes and
place them on the salt bed—they should all fit in the pan without
touching each other. Place in the oven and bake for 1 to 1¼ hours or until
the potatoes are tender.

Remove the potatoes from the oven and allow to cool for 5 minutes
or until you can handle them—you might need a towel or gloves to hold
the potatoes. Cut them in half and scoop the cooked potato out of the
skins. Pass the potato flesh through a food mill or hand ricer and put it
into a measuring cup.

For every cup of warm riced potato measured out, use 1 cup (125 g)
sifted flour and 1 egg yolk. Season with salt and truffles, then mix for
30 seconds to 1 minute until a soft dough forms.

Cut the ball of dough in half (or, if it's easier for you, quarters). On a
well-floured surface, roll each piece of dough into a long rope about
½ inch (1 cm) in diameter. Cut into ½-inch (1 cm) long pieces.

You can prepare the gnocchi a few hours ahead to this point.
Arrange them on a well-floured baking sheet and chill until you're
ready to cook them.

When you're ready to serve the gnocchi, bring a large pot of salted
water to a boil and drop the gnocchi into the water. They're ready when
they float to the top; this should take only a couple of minutes. Scoop the
gnocchi out with a spider or strainer, then toss in butter and olive oil.
Season with salt and sprinkle with parsley and pecorino romano cheese.

Chef Springett created this lemony potato salad to accompany his foie gras and smoked salmon terrine (page 174), but it would make a zingy side to simply seared salmon or halibut as well. Fingerling potatoes are heritage cultivars that grow small and narrow and are more flavourful than many commercial varieties. That said, if they are unavailable, you can always use any small nugget potato instead.

FINGERLING POTATO SALAD

PREPARE THE POTATOES: In a pot of salted water, place the potatoes and bring to a boil, then cover and simmer until tender, about 15 minutes. Remove from the heat and cool to room temperature.

MAKE THE LEMON DRESSING: Whisk the egg yolks together with the lemon juice, zest, mustard, and honey, then slowly whisk in the oil. Season with salt and cayenne and adjust the other seasonings to taste.

Slice the fingerling potatoes, then combine with the radishes, shallots, dill, and chives. Toss with the lemon dressing, setting some aside if needed as a garnish.

SALAD

1 lb (450 g) fingerling potatoes
3 red radishes, halved, thinly
   sliced, and soaked in ice water
2 medium shallots, thinly sliced
Dill sprigs to taste
Chives, finely sliced, to taste
Salt to taste

LEMON DRESSING

2 egg yolks
Juice of 2 lemons
Finely grated zest of 1 lemon
1 tsp (5 mL) Dijon mustard
½ Tbsp (7 mL) honey
7 Tbsp (105 mL) grapeseed oil, or
   as needed
Salt and cayenne pepper to taste

**MAKES 10 SMALL
PORTIONS**

*"The Wickaninnish Inn taught me to cook with the ingredients that surround you . . .
a philosophy of cooking that has stuck with me to this very day."*

Chef Profile: **DUNCAN LY**

AFTER HIGH SCHOOL, Duncan Ly headed to Tofino to follow his life's passion: learning how to surf. To make some extra money, he took a summer job washing dishes at the Wickaninnish Inn, and it changed everything. "I remember watching the chefs working and seeing beautifully plated food coming off the line," he recalls. "That was when I made the decision that one day I would become a chef."

Most of all, Chef Ly remembers the incredibly fresh local seafood: albacore tuna, octopus, live scallops, gooseneck barnacles, and Oyster Jim's giant beach oysters. "Long before it became trendy, the Wickaninnish Inn taught me to cook with the ingredients that surround you and cook with seasonal ingredients—a philosophy of cooking that has stuck with me to this very day," Chef Ly says.

Over the next two years, he graduated from dishwasher to apprentice and worked on almost every station. Eventually, he moved back to the city, cooking at Vancouver's Diva at the Met and Calgary's Catch before joining the Hotel Arts Group as executive chef overseeing Raw Bar, Yellow Door Bistro, and Chef's Table at Kensington Riverside Inn, Calgary's first Relais & Châteaux property. Along the way he won numerous awards, including a silver medal at the 2014 Canadian Culinary Championships. In 2016, he opened his first restaurant, the Pan-Asian Foreign Concept, to rave reviews.

◀ *Chef Ly's Seared Albacore Tuna with Marinated Shiitake Mushrooms and Wakame Salad (recipe on page 128)*

To End the Day

▼

DESSERTS

THE SUN SINKS toward the horizon, bathing everything in a wash of rosy gold. The ocean seems purple in this light, the wavelets of the evening tide gilded. The last surfers ride the sun's path to the shore. Shadows lengthen. Darkness falls and the first stars glimmer against a sky that shifts from blue to pink to orange to violet.

Every time of day is beautiful here on Chesterman Beach, but the most extraordinary moments are just at the day's end. You could say the same for the cuisine.

The Inn's pastry chefs have always brought a passion for fine ingredients and a meticulous attention to detail to their tarts and tortes, mousses and macarons. Some, like Chef Conradi, indulged guests with ornate chocolatey delight. Others, like Chef Wilson, took an innovatively modern approach to comforting favourites like apple pie. Innovation and tradition meet sweetly here, creating something fine to end the day.

Today's team is as likely to find sweet inspiration in the woods and fields as they are in their European training. That could mean a sorbet made with tiny purple Oregon grapes or lichen that's been candied and used as a garnish. As it has been since the beginning, as much as possible is made in-house, from the ice creams to the tart shells to the sauces. In the hands of the Inn's pastry chefs, every dinner ends with a work of art as delicious to look at as it is to eat.

Shadows lengthen. Darkness falls and the first stars glimmer against a sky that shifts from blue to pink to orange to violet.

Chef Conradi knows what chocolate lovers want: this rich, dark, dense cake with its warm, gooey, molten chocolate centre. When he was at the Inn, he served it as part of his decadent chocolate platter for two (photo opposite).

MOELLEUX (Molten Chocolate Cake)

4 eggs
¾ cup (150 g) sugar
1¼ cups (160 g) flour
1½ tsp (7.5 g) baking powder
8 oz (225 g) dark chocolate,
  chopped
1 cup (230 g) butter, softened

MAKES 6 SMALL CAKES

Preheat the oven to 375°F (190°C). Butter six medium-size ramekins, then dust with a little sugar. Arrange on a rimmed baking sheet.

In a large bowl, whisk the eggs and sugar lightly together.

In a second, smaller bowl, sift the flour and baking powder together.

Place a metal bowl over a pot of boiling water and add the chocolate and butter. Cook, stirring constantly, until the chocolate has melted and combined with the butter into a smooth cream.

Slowly whisk the melted chocolate into the beaten eggs, a little at a time to start with to temper the eggs. Mix well, then fold in the flour mixture.

Divide the batter between the ramekins and bake for about 10 minutes or until the tops are cooked but the insides are still a little gooey. Cool for a few minutes, then run a knife around the edges of the cakes to loosen them and invert them onto a plate.

The cakes are best served slightly warm. If you like, serve with the Tahitian vanilla ice cream (page 230) and/or raspberry purée (page 271).

INN-STYLE

Pastry Chef Conradi's favourite dessert was the chocolate platter for two, photographed opposite. He designed it to be a mini chocolate buffet for two people. It comprised all the rich favourites people love: chocolate-covered strawberries, served alongside Moelleux (recipe above), chocolate fondue (page 200), chocolate mousse (page 201), chocolate parfait (page 201), bitter chocolate raspberry ice cream (page 232), and raspberry purée (page 271). Each of these makes an exquisite dessert on its own, but for a showstopping dinner-party finale, why not present all of them together?

What could be more romantic than sharing this dessert created by Pastry Chef Conradi? Dark, rich, silky melted chocolate with bits of fruit or cake for dipping— it's interactive dining at its best.

CHOCOLATE FONDUE

⅜ cup (100 mL) milk

2 Tbsp (30 mL) honey

4 oz (110 g) dark chocolate, chopped

1½ Tbsp (20 g) butter, cut into small pieces

¼ cup (60 mL) cream

Pieces of fruit or cake, for dipping

SERVES 2

In a small pot over medium heat, bring the milk and honey to a boil. Add the chopped chocolate and stir until completely melted. Mix in the butter while stirring constantly.

Whip the cream and fold into the fondue. Keep warm—a fondue pot over a small flame is ideal for this—and serve with pieces of fruit or cake for dipping.

Pastry Chef Conradi makes this mousse with sweet, subtle white chocolate, which is delicious topped with fresh berries. If you prefer to go deeper, however, you could use milk or dark chocolate instead. It's a great make-ahead dessert, best served in pretty vessels such as vintage wine glasses.

WHITE CHOCOLATE MOUSSE

In a heatproof bowl over a pot of boiling water, melt the chocolate.

In a separate bowl, whisk the eggs with the sugar until light and creamy.

Stir the gelatin into the warm chocolate until fully dissolved. Stir in the kirsch.

Whisk a little warm white chocolate into the egg mixture to temper it, then slowly add the rest. Mix well.

Whip the cream, then fold it into the chocolate and egg mixture.

Spoon the mousse into ramekins or glasses and keep chilled until you're ready to serve.

18 oz (500 g) white chocolate, chopped
2 eggs
Pinch of sugar
6 sheets gelatin, rehydrated, or 1 Tbsp (12 g) powdered gelatin
3 Tbsp (45 mL) kirsch
5 cups (1.25 mL) whipping cream

SERVES 6 TO 8

Parfait? Perfect! Like a chocolate mousse, this dessert created by Pastry Chef Conradi is at once light and airy yet creamy and rich. The parfait, though, is frozen for an added element of chilly elegance. It's perfectly delicious served with just a whisper of raspberry purée (page 271).

WHITE CHOCOLATE PARFAIT

Line four to six small freezer-safe moulds with plastic wrap, letting the plastic wrap hang over the sides to make it easier to remove the parfait later.

In a heatproof mixing bowl over a pot of boiling water, melt the white chocolate. Remove from the heat.

In a separate bowl, whisk the egg yolks and egg white together with the vanilla seeds and sugar. Add a little warm chocolate to the eggs and whisk it in to temper the eggs. Then slowly add the rest of the chocolate, mixing well. Add the Grand Marnier.

Whip the cream until it is fairly firm, then fold it into the chocolate and egg mixture.

Spoon the mixture into the prepared moulds, smooth the tops, and freeze for several hours or overnight. When you're ready to serve, lift the parfaits out using the plastic wrap, invert onto a plate, and remove the wrap.

7 oz (200 g) white chocolate, chopped
3 egg yolks
1 egg white
Scraped-out seeds of ½ vanilla bean
1 Tbsp (10 g) sugar
2 tsp (10 mL) Grand Marnier
2¼ cups (550 mL) whipping cream

SERVES 4 TO 6

Magic happens when chocolate, caramel, and salt come together. Add a buttery chocolate sablé base, and you have this addictive tart, both sophisticated and yet oh, so easy to love.

SALTED CARAMEL and CHOCOLATE TART

GLUTEN-FREE CHOCOLATE SABLÉ DOUGH

⅞ cup (200 g) butter, room temperature

⅞ cup (100 g) icing sugar

2 egg yolks, room temperature

1⅔ cups (225 g) Cup4Cup Gluten Free Multipurpose Flour

⅓ cup (25 g) cocoa powder

1 tsp (3 g) salt

CARAMEL

½ cup (125 mL) whipping cream

1 cup (230 g) butter

1⅓ cups (293 g) brown sugar

Pinch of salt

½ tsp (2 mL) vanilla extract

CHOCOLATE GANACHE

1¼ cups (215 g) chopped (small chunks) 62% chocolate

1 cup (250 mL) whipping cream

ASSEMBLY

Sea salt (optional)

Cocoa nibs (optional)

MAKES 6 TARTS

MAKE THE SABLÉ DOUGH: In the bowl of a stand mixer fitted with a paddle attachment, cream the butter and icing sugar together. Slowly add the yolks one by one with the mixer running; blend well after each addition and scrape down the sides of the bowl occasionally.

Meanwhile, in a separate bowl, mix the dry ingredients together, then slowly add them to the butter mixture, mixing well. Form the dough into a thick disc, wrap in plastic wrap, and rest in the refrigerator for about an hour.

Preheat the oven to 350°F (180°C).

Between sheets of parchment paper, roll out the dough to ¼ inch (6 mm) thickness. Cut into six circles large enough to fit into six small tart pans, 4 inches (about 10 cm) in diameter and preferably with removable bottoms, and transfer to the pans.

Stab the bottom of each tart shell with a fork, then place the tart pans on a baking sheet. Blind-bake for 12 minutes (see note on page 203). Remove the plastic wrap or parchment and pie weights and bake for another 4 minutes, rotating once. The bottom of the tart shells should be firm to the touch. Remove from the oven and cool completely.

MAKE THE CARAMEL: In a saucepan, place the cream, butter, and brown sugar and clip a candy thermometer to the side. Bring to a boil over medium heat and continue to cook until the caramel reaches 234°F (112°C). Remove from the heat, then stir in the salt and vanilla.

PREPARE THE CHOCOLATE GANACHE: Place the chocolate chunks in a heatproof bowl. In a small pot, heat the cream just to a simmer, then pour overtop the chocolate and whisk hard until emulsified.

TO ASSEMBLE: Pour a little caramel into each tart shell, then top with the chocolate ganache. If you like, sprinkle a little sea salt and some cocoa nibs on top. For a truly spectacular finish, as shown in the photo opposite, you can also add chocolate cookie crumbs, rich chocolate ice cream (page 233), chocolate truffles, and sea foam candy.

BLIND-BAKING

Blind-baking is the process of baking an empty tart or pie shell so you can fill it later with a custard or other unbaked filling. The trick is to weight down the pastry dough to prevent the bottom of the crust from bubbling up to form air pockets, and at the same time, keep the delicate pastry from burning. Here's how to do it: Line a tart or pie pan with pastry dough, trimming to fit, then stab the bottom of the dough a few times with a fork. Line the dough-lined pan with parchment paper, and fill with pie weights to preserve the shape of the shell while baking. The pie weights can be dried beans, rice, or specially purchased ceramic pie weights. Place the pan on a baking sheet, then blind-bake at 350°F (180°C) for 12 to 15 minutes. Remove the weights and parchment and bake for another 4 to 5 minutes, rotating once if necessary. The edge of the shell should be golden brown and the bottom firm to the touch. Remove from the oven and cool completely before filling.

At the Inn, this rich, decadent chocolate dessert comes dressed with chocolate ice cream, crispy cookies called dentelles, candied hazelnuts, and candied lichen. You can recreate this showstopping masterpiece at home, or you can keep it simple with layers of nutty dacquoise layered with a luxuriously creamy filling.

CHOCOLATE and HAZELNUT DESSERT

HAZELNUT DACQUOISE

4 egg whites

¾ cup (150 g) sugar

1¼ cups (150 g) icing sugar

1½ cups (145 g) ground hazelnuts, toasted

3 Tbsp (25 g) corn starch

CHOCOLATE CRÉMEUX

⅓ cup (80 mL) chilled whipping cream, plus 1½ cups (375 mL) whipping cream

⅓ cup (80 mL) milk

2 egg yolks

1 Tbsp (10 g) sugar

1 sheet gelatin, rehydrated, or ½ tsp (2 g) powdered gelatin

11 oz (315 g) 64% chocolate, melted

3½ oz (100 g) hazelnut butter

ASSEMBLY

Optional for serving: Cocoa nib dentelles (page 233), candied hazelnuts (page 265), candied lichen (page 266), and chocolate ice cream (page 233)

SERVES 6

MAKE THE HAZELNUT DACQUOISE: Preheat the oven to 300°F (150°C). Line a large baking sheet with parchment paper.

In the bowl of a stand mixer, whip the egg whites until soft peaks form. Slowly add the sugar and continue to mix on low speed for 30 seconds.

In a separate bowl, sift together the remaining ingredients, then fold into the egg whites. Scrape into a piping bag fitted with a large round tip, then pipe concentric circles of the mixture onto the parchment-lined baking sheet. Start from the centre as you pipe them and make the circles about 2 inches (5 cm) wide. This recipe should make about 20 discs.

Place in the oven and bake for 12 to 15 minutes or until crisp on the outside and still tender in the centre. Remove from the oven and cool completely.

MAKE THE CHOCOLATE CRÉMEUX: In a pot over medium heat, combine the ⅓ cup (80 mL) chilled whipping cream with the milk and bring to a simmer, taking care not to burn the milk on the bottom of the pot. Remove from the heat and turn the burner to low.

In a medium-size heatproof bowl, place the egg yolks and sugar, then slowly whisk the hot milk mixture into the egg yolks. Return the mixture to the pot. Stirring constantly to avoid curdling the eggs, bring the mixture to 183°F (84°C). Once the mixture has come to temperature and is nice and thick, remove it from the heat and strain it into a bowl.

In a clean small pot, bring the remaining 1½ cups (375 mL) whipping cream just to a simmer. Stir the gelatin into the warm custard, then add the hot cream. Place the chocolate and hazelnut butter in a heatproof bowl, then pour the warm custard and cream mixture overtop to melt the chocolate and hazelnut butter completely. Whisk to ensure it all comes together, then cool to room temperature and transfer to a piping bag.

For each dessert, you will need three discs of dacquoise. Pipe a generous layer of the chocolate crémeux onto two of the discs, then stack them to form a sandwich, topped with the third disc. Pipe dollops of crémeux onto each plate, using one of the dollops to secure a stack of filled dacquoise. If you like, garnish each serving with a cocoa nib dentelle, candied hazelnuts, and candied lichen, then finish with a scoop of chocolate ice cream.

Chef Butters's richly chocolatey dessert keeps the gluten-free guests happy, while the rest won't even notice the difference. He suggests serving this with warm chocolate sauce, raspberry compote, and raspberry sorbet, but you can also top it with fresh raspberries and whipped cream.

DOUBLE-CHOCOLATE MASHED-POTATO BRIOCHE

5 oz (150 g) bittersweet chocolate, chopped

1 Tbsp (4 g) instant coffee granules

3 Tbsp (45 mL) amaretto

½ cup (115 g) butter

4 eggs, room temperature, separated

½ cup (100 g) sugar

1 cup (250 mL) mashed potatoes, preferably russet, drained and fairly dry

½ cup (50 g) finely ground almonds

Pinch of salt

½ cup (85 g) chocolate chips, preferably milk chocolate

Optional toppings: chocolate sauce, raspberry compote or coulis, fresh raspberries, whipped cream, raspberry sorbet

SERVES 6 TO 8

Preheat the oven to 350°F (180°C). Grease eight small brioche moulds or six large muffin cups.

In a heatproof bowl set over a double boiler, melt the bittersweet chocolate, coffee, amaretto, and butter. Cool for a minute or two.

In a separate bowl, beat the egg yolks with the sugar until thick and creamy. Add the melted chocolate mixture to the yolk mixture and stir. Add the mashed potatoes and ground almonds and stir until thoroughly combined.

In an immaculately clean mixing bowl, beat the egg whites until stiff, then fold into the chocolate and potato mixture. Gently fold in the salt and chocolate chips.

Spoon into the brioche moulds or muffin cups and place in the oven. Bake for approximately 30 minutes or until a wooden skewer inserted in the centre comes out clean. Let cool for 15 minutes before removing from the moulds.

Serve alongside chocolate or raspberry sauce, fresh berries, and whipped cream or if you prefer, raspberry sorbet or chocolate ice cream.

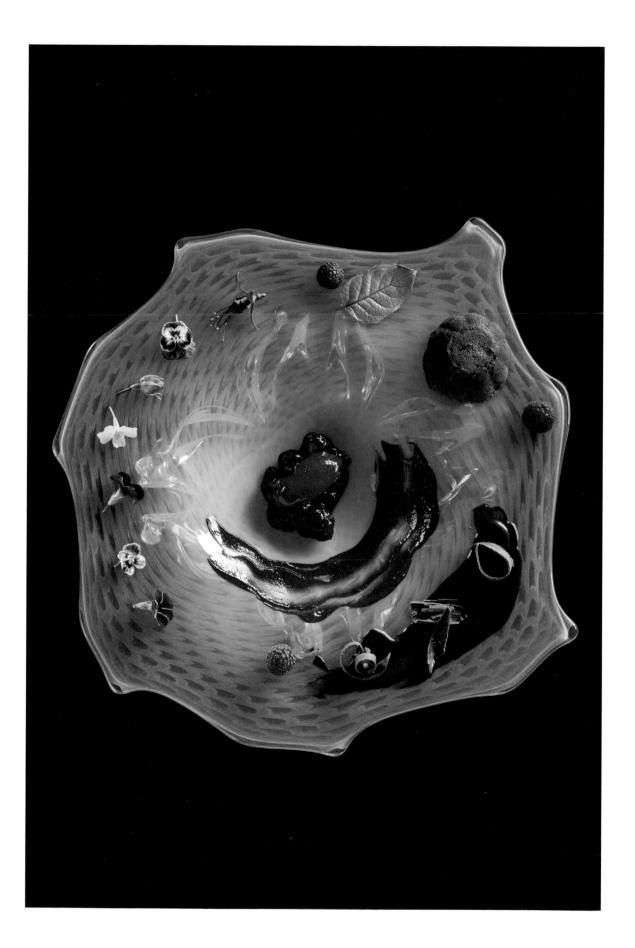

Tender, moist, and lemony—Pastry Chef Wilson's olive oil cake is like a pound cake, but even better. It's perfect with a cup of tea and best enjoyed while watching the waves outside the window at the Wickaninnish Inn.

OLIVE OIL CAKE

CAKE

3 Tbsp (45 mL) invert sugar or
   light corn syrup (see note)
4 eggs
⅞ cup (175 g) sugar
1¾ cups (220 g) flour
2 tsp (10 g) baking powder
½ tsp (2 g) salt
Finely grated zest of 1 lemon
⅞ cup (200 mL) olive oil

LEMON SYRUP

1 cup (200 g) sugar
1 cup (250 mL) water
1½ cups (375 mL) lemon juice

LEMON GLAZE

3 to 4 Tbsp (45 to 60 mL) lemon
   juice
2 cups (240 g) icing sugar

MAKES 2 LOAVES

Preheat the oven to 350°F (180°C) and line two large loaf pans with parchment paper.

In a food processor, place the invert sugar (or corn syrup) and eggs and blend until the mixture is light and frothy. (Alternatively, you can use a stand mixer fitted with a paddle attachment.) Once the mixture starts to get fluffy, slowly stream in the sugar and continue to blend until almost white.

In a separate bowl, mix together the flour, baking powder, and salt, then sift twice to make sure everything is well combined. Slowly pour the dry ingredients into the food processor, add the lemon zest, and process until everything is combined. Continue to process and slowly add in the olive oil until fully emulsified.

Scrape the batter into the parchment-lined loaf pans and bake for 20 to 25 minutes or until golden brown and a wooden skewer inserted into the cake comes out clean.

While the cake is baking, make the lemon syrup: In a small pot, bring the sugar and water just to a boil, stirring often, until the sugar is fully dissolved. Pour into a heatproof bowl and allow to cool to room temperature. Stir in the lemon juice. (The lemon syrup can be made ahead of time and will keep for several weeks in the refrigerator.)

Remove the loaves from the oven and brush with the lemon syrup while still hot. Allow to cool completely.

Make the lemon glaze: Whisk the lemon juice and icing sugar together until fully blended. The glaze should be thick but still pourable. If necessary, add more sugar or lemon juice until you reach the desired consistency. Drizzle the glaze over the cooled loaves and allow to set for about an hour before slicing and serving.

INVERT SUGAR

Ever wondered why your baked goods don't turn out the way they do at your favourite bakery? That's because pastry chefs have some clever tricks up their white sleeves—tools like ice cream stabilizers, gelatin sheets, and invert sugar. The last is a syrup used in confectionery, patisserie, and ice cream to prevent crystallization, give foods a tender mouthfeel, and increase the browning effect. The best-known brand name is Trimoline; unfortunately, it's not readily available to home cooks. You can use an equal amount of light corn syrup as a substitute.

Thyme and blueberry, it turns out, were meant for each other. The subtle savoury spice of the herb perfectly complements the sweet tartness of the blueberries. Executive Chef Barr's elegant tart marries these complex flavours with a mild lemon curd and buttery sablé crust.

BLUEBERRY and THYME TART

SABLÉ DOUGH

1 cup (230 g) butter, room
    temperature
¾ cup (90 g) icing sugar
2 egg yolks, room temperature
2 cups (250 g) flour
1 tsp (3 g) salt
Finely grated zest of 1 lemon
1 sprig thyme, leaves only,
    chopped

THYME OIL

1¼ cups (300 mL) grapeseed oil
8 sprigs thyme, leaves only
1 bunch parsley, leaves only

LEMON CURD

¾ cup (185 mL) lemon juice,
    about 4 lemons
4 eggs, room temperature
½ cup (100 g) sugar
2 Tbsp (30 mL) honey
1 cup (230 g) butter, room
    temperature

ASSEMBLY

1 lb (450 g) fresh blueberries
¼ cup (60 mL) maple syrup
Flowering thyme, for garnish
    (optional)

MAKES 6 TARTS

MAKE THE SABLÉ DOUGH: In the bowl of a stand mixer, cream the butter and icing sugar together. Slowly add the egg yolks. Once well incorporated, add the dry ingredients, lemon zest, and thyme. Roll the dough into a ball, then flatten into a disc, wrap in plastic wrap, and rest in the refrigerator for at least 2 hours or overnight.

On a well-floured surface, roll out the dough about ¼ inch (6 mm) thick. Cut the dough into six pieces to line six small tart pans, 4 inches (10 cm) in diameter and preferably with removable bottoms. Stab the dough with a fork, then place the tart shells on a baking sheet and rest in the refrigerator for 45 minutes.

Preheat the oven to 375°F (190°C). Blind-bake the dough for 15 minutes (see note on page 203); remove the parchment paper and the pie weights, then bake for 5 more minutes or until the edges are golden and the bottom is firm. Remove from the oven and cool.

MAKE THE THYME OIL: In a blender, place all of the ingredients and blend on high speed until the jug is warm to the touch. Strain through cheesecloth into a bowl set over ice.

MAKE THE LEMON CURD: Fill a large pot with a couple of inches (about 5 cm) of water and bring to a simmer. In a heatproof bowl that fits over the pot, place the lemon juice, eggs, sugar, and honey and whisk constantly until thickened. Remove from the heat and stir in the butter until incorporated.

TO ASSEMBLE: Spread the lemon curd in the bottom of the tart shells. Toss the blueberries in the maple syrup and 2 Tbsp (30 mL) thyme oil. (The remaining oil can be used to garnish the plates or reserved for other uses, such as salad dressings.) Place the blueberries in an even layer over the lemon curd in each tart shell, pressing gently, until the curd is completely covered. If you like, drizzle some of the excess maple syrup and thyme oil from the blueberries over and around the tarts and garnish with thyme flowers. A small dollop of Oregon grape sorbet (page 236) makes a nice complement to this.

What could be better than apples cooked in caramel and topped with a crisp, cinnamon-dusted coronet of filo pastry? This irresistible dessert created by Pastry Chef Conradi is a luxurious way to end a special meal. Best of all, all the components can be made ahead of time and assembled at the last minute for a truly impressive grand finale.

APPLE CROUSTADE

BUTTER-POACHED APPLES

1 cup (230 g) butter

1½ cups (300 g) sugar

6 Granny Smith apples, peeled, halved, and cored

1½ cups (375 mL) cream

FILO CORONETS

¼ cup (50 g) sugar

½ tsp (1 g) ground cinnamon

6 sheets frozen filo dough, thawed

½ cup (115 g) butter, melted and clarified

SERVES 6

PREPARE THE BUTTER-POACHED APPLES: In a large skillet over medium heat, melt the butter, stir in the sugar, and cook until lightly caramelized. The caramel should be a light amber colour; take care not to let it get too dark or it will be bitter. This should take only a few minutes.

Place the apples cut side down in the caramel and cook until they start to caramelize on the bottom.

Turn the apples over and caramelize on the outside, taking care not to overcook them. Remove from the pan and place on a wire rack to cool.

Whisk the cream into the hot caramel, taking care not to let the mixture splash or boil again. Strain the caramel cream and place it in the refrigerator. Chill the apples and sauce for a couple of hours before using.

MAKE THE FILO CORONETS: Preheat the oven to 400°F (200°C).

Mix together the sugar and cinnamon. Brush each filo sheet with butter and sprinkle with the cinnamon sugar.

Form each sheet into a rough crown shape (or, if you prefer, fold each into the cavity of a muffin tin to form a filo cup). Bake for 10 to 15 minutes or until crisp and golden.

TO SERVE: Cut the apples into wedges and heat with some of the apple-caramel sauce. Garnish with a filo coronet or place apples inside a filo cup. Serve with Tahitian vanilla ice cream (page 230).

Technically, this is not a traditional apple pie. Chef Wilson's version is a deconstructed take of delicate apple compote topped with buttery sablé crumble. Sablés are traditional French butter cookies with a slightly sandy texture—"sablé" means sandy—and are even better than your usual pie crust. Prefer your pie topped with ice cream or cheddar cheese? How about both? Add the whimsy of cheddar ice cream apples (page 216) for a stunning dessert. Note that you will need a vacuum sealer to make the compressed apples.

APPLE PIE

COMPRESSED APPLES
½ cup (100 g) sugar
½ cup (125 mL) white wine
½ cup (125 mL) water
2 Granny Smith apples

SABLÉ DOUGH
4 cups (500 g) flour
1⅔ cups (200 g) icing sugar
1¾ cups (400 g) butter, room temperature
4 egg yolks, room temperature

APPLE COMPOTE
4 apples, preferably Pink Lady
¼ cup (60 g) butter
¼ cup (50 g) sugar
1 tsp (2 g) ground cinnamon

SERVES 4 TO 6

MAKE THE COMPRESSED APPLES: Bring the sugar, wine, and water to a boil, then remove from the heat and allow to cool.

Using a mandoline, slice the apples paper-thin. Place them into a vacuum-sealer bag and add ¼ cup (60 mL) of the cooled liquid, then compress the apples in a vacuum sealer. Allow to sit for 6 hours or until they are transparent and bright green.

MAKE THE SABLÉ DOUGH: In the bowl of a stand mixer fitted with a dough hook, place the flour, icing sugar, and butter and mix on low speed until the mixture resembles bread crumbs, then add the egg yolks. Continue mixing until a dough forms. Remove the dough and shape and pat into a thick square, then place in the fridge to rest for 2 hours.

MAKE THE COMPOTE: Peel and core the apples, then cut them into ½-inch (1 cm) cubes. In a frying pan, heat the butter until it almost clarifies. Add the apples and toss until just tender. Stir in the sugar and cinnamon until well distributed, then remove from the heat and cool until needed.

BAKE THE SABLÉ DOUGH: Preheat the oven to 350°F (180°C). Roll out the sablé dough until it is ½ inch (1 cm) thick. Place on a baking sheet lined with parchment paper and bake until golden brown, about 12 to 15 minutes. Set aside until cool.

TO ASSEMBLE: Dollop a line of the apple compote down the centre of each plate. Crush up some of the baked sablé dough and cover the compote. Take the compressed apples out of the vacuum-sealer bag, drain off excess liquid, and arrange them over the sablé crumble until it is covered. If you like, serve with a cheddar ice cream apple (page 216).

Whimsical yet sophisticated, Chef Wilson's ice cream spheres add a savoury tang of cheddar to the frozen dessert. Charming alongside a slice of apple pie (or the deconstructed version, page 214), these also make a sweet treat on their own. Note that for this recipe, you will need an ice cream maker and half-mould spheres, which you can find at bakery supply stores.

CHEDDAR ICE CREAM APPLES

CHEDDAR ICE CREAM

1⅓ cups (330 mL) skim milk

1 cup (250 mL) cream

4 egg yolks

⅜ cup (75 g) sugar

1 cup (110 g) grated sharp cheddar
   cheese

½ tsp (2 g) salt

DECORATIONS

1 cup (220 g) cocoa butter

1 tsp (4 g) green powder colour

1 oz (30 g) milk chocolate, or as
   needed

MAKES ABOUT 1 DOZEN

MAKE THE CHEDDAR ICE CREAM: In a saucepan, bring the milk and cream to a boil.

While waiting for the milk and cream to boil, mix the yolks and sugar together in a bowl. Once the milk and cream have come to a boil, slowly add them to the yolk mixture, whisking constantly. Pour the mixture back into the saucepan, return to low heat, and cook until the custard is thick enough to coat the back of a spoon. For the greatest accuracy, and to avoid overcooking, use a thermometer—the custard should reach 170°F (85°C).

Immediately take off the heat and whisk in the grated cheddar cheese and salt, stirring until all the cheese is melted. Pass through a fine-mesh strainer and cool it in a bowl set over an ice bath. Once cold, place the mixture into an ice cream maker and freeze according to the manufacturer's instructions.

Scoop the ice cream into small half-sphere moulds and freeze for another 12 hours. Remove the half spheres from the moulds and put them together to create full spheres. Place on a tray and return to the freezer to firm up.

DECORATE AND FINISH THE SPHERES: In a heatproof bowl set over a pot of boiling water, melt the cocoa butter and green powder colour and mix well. Take the ice cream spheres out of the freezer; place a metal skewer in the end of one of the spheres and dip into the liquid cocoa butter mixture. Place onto a tray and return to the freezer. Repeat with the remaining spheres.

Melt some milk chocolate and place in a piping bag. Pipe little stems onto a piece of parchment paper and attach to the spheres to make them resemble little apple stalks. Store on a parchment-lined tray in the freezer until needed.

Buttery sablé crust topped with spicy apple butter and tender sautéed apples—these little apple tartlets make the perfect sweet finish for a party. You can make them bite-size and buffet-ready as we do at the Inn, or, if you prefer, use a slightly larger tart pan for a sit-down dessert.

APPLE TART PETIT FOURS

MAKE THE SABLÉ TART SHELLS: In a stand mixer fitted with a paddle attachment, cream the butter and icing sugar together on medium speed until smooth and light. Add the egg yolks one at a time, mixing well after each addition. Once well incorporated, turn the speed to low and slowly add the flour and salt.

Form the dough into a thick disc and cover with plastic wrap. Chill in the refrigerator for at least 1 hour.

Preheat the oven to 375°F (190°C) and line a large baking sheet with parchment paper.

On a well-floured surface, roll out the dough to ¼ inch (6 mm) thick. Cut the dough into 12 circles big enough to fit into small tart pans or ring moulds, about 2½ inches (6 cm) in diameter. Line the tart pans or ring moulds with the dough and place them on the baking sheet. Blind-bake for 12 minutes (see note on page 203); remove the pie weights, including the parchment paper, then bake for 5 more minutes or until the edges are golden and the bottom is firm. Remove from the oven and cool.

MAKE THE FILLING: In a small pan over medium heat, cook the sugar and cinnamon until they melt, then add the diced apples and cook until just softened and lightly caramelized.

MAKE THE CHANTILLY CREAM: Using an electric mixer, whisk together the cream, icing sugar, and vanilla and continue beating at medium-high speed until soft peaks form. Chill until needed.

TO ASSEMBLE: Fill the tart shells halfway with apple butter, then top them with the sautéed apples. Allow to cool, then top each tart with a dollop of Chantilly cream.

SABLÉ TART SHELLS
1 cup (230 g) butter, room temperature
¾ cup (90 g) icing sugar
2 egg yolks, room temperature
2 cups (250 g) flour
1 tsp (3 g) salt

FILLING
2 Tbsp (25 g) sugar
1½ tsp (3 g) ground cinnamon
2 green apples, peeled, cored, and diced small
1 cup (250 mL) apple butter (page 271)

CHANTILLY CREAM
1 cup (250 mL) cream
2 Tbsp (14 g) icing sugar
½ tsp (2 mL) vanilla extract

MAKES ABOUT 12 TARTLETS

When the Inn throws a party, these sweet treats are always a big hit. A simple carrot cake base is spiced up with a generous amount of cinnamon and elevated with a drizzle of lemon icing glaze topped with a candied pecan. Of course, if you don't want to cut it into bite-size pieces, you can always offer more generous portions instead.

CARROT CAKE PETIT FOURS

2 cups (250 g) flour
1 tsp (5 g) baking soda
2 tsp (10 g) baking powder
½ tsp (2 g) salt
2 tsp (4 g) ground cinnamon
4 eggs
1½ cups (330 g) brown sugar
1 tsp (5 mL) vanilla extract
1 cup (250 mL) vegetable oil
2 cups (220 g) grated carrots
   (about 2 large)
Lemon icing glaze (recipe below)
Candied pecans (page 266),
   chopped

SERVES A CROWD

Preheat the oven to 375°F (190°C). Line a 9- × 13-inch (23 × 33 cm) baking pan with parchment paper or non-stick aluminum foil, making sure the corners fit tightly and allowing the edges to hang over the sides of the pan to make removal easier.

In a large bowl, sift together the flour, baking soda, baking powder, salt, and cinnamon.

In a separate, smaller bowl, whisk the eggs together with the sugar and vanilla; add the oil and whisk until well blended.

Using a wooden spoon, stir the wet ingredients into the dry ones, making sure there are no floury patches left. Gently fold in the carrots.

Scrape into the prepared pan and bake for about 40 minutes or until the top is lightly golden and a wooden skewer inserted into the centre comes out dry. Remove from the pan and allow to cool.

Slice into long bite-size pieces, then drizzle the tops with the lemon icing glaze and finish with chopped candied pecans on each piece.

Lemon Icing Glaze

1½ cups (180 g) icing sugar
Finely grated zest of 2 lemons
2 to 3 Tbsp (30 to 45 mL) lemon
   juice

**MAKES ABOUT 1 CUP
(250 ML)**

Stir together the icing sugar and lemon zest, then stir in the lemon juice, adding a little at a time until it is still fairly thick but liquid enough to drizzle.

Apple Tart Petit Fours (page 217), Carrot Cake Petit Fours (page 220), macarons (similar recipe, page 222), and Burnt-Honey Gelées with Goat Cheese Mousse (page 224) ▶

Like rubies, these brilliantly red petit fours are vivid little gems filled with a luxurious chocolate and raspberry-flavoured ganache. The beet powder adds colour and sweet earthiness to the macarons; just remember to make the powder ahead of time for a sweet treat your dinner guests will be talking about for months to come.

BEET and RASPBERRY MACARONS

MACARONS
2⅓ cups (280 g) icing sugar

3 cups (300 g) almond flour

2 Tbsp (15 g) beet powder
   (page 275)

½ tsp (2 g) salt

6 egg whites

1½ cups (300 g) sugar

⅓ cup (80 mL) water

GANACHE
3⅓ cups (567 g) chopped (small
   chunks) dark chocolate

1 cup (250 mL) cream

1 cup (250 mL) raspberry purée
   (page 271)

SERVES A CROWD

MAKE THE MACARONS: Preheat the oven to 275°F (135°C) and line two baking sheets with parchment paper.

Into a medium-size bowl, sift the icing sugar, almond flour, beet powder, and salt.

Place three of the egg whites into the bowl of a stand mixer fitted with a whip attachment.

Clip a candy thermometer to the side of a small pot, place over medium heat, and add the sugar and water. When the syrup reaches 239°F (115°C), start whipping the three egg whites on high.

Once the syrup reaches 244°F (118°C), remove from the heat and slowly pour down the side of the stand-mixer bowl as the machine continues to whip the egg whites. Whip until the bottom of the bowl is just warm.

Pour the remaining three egg whites into the almond-flour mixture and mix well. Using a rubber spatula, fold in a third of the beaten egg-white meringue mixture; mix well until you have a uniform paste. Fold in the rest of the meringue a third at a time, mixing well before adding the next round.

Scoop the mixture into a piping bag fitted with a small round tip, and shake down to get out as many bubbles as possible.

Pipe a bit of the mixture beneath each corner of the parchment on the baking sheets to prevent the corners from flying up in the oven. Then pipe small rounds on the parchment, about 1 to 1½ inches (2.5 to 4 cm) in diameter and about 2 inches (5 cm) apart. Tap the sheets on a table a few times to remove all bubbles.

With the oven door slightly ajar, bake for 4 minutes, then rotate the sheets and bake for another 4 minutes, still leaving the door ajar. Check the doneness by jiggling the macarons. If they are still jiggly and not yet set, rotate the sheets again and bake for another minute or two. Cool completely before filling.

MAKE THE GANACHE: Place the chocolate chunks into a heatproof bowl. In a small pot, bring the cream and raspberry purée to a boil. Pour overtop the chocolate and whisk to combine. Scoop into a piping bag fitted with a small round tip and pipe a little ganache on the flat side of half the baked macaron shells; top with the other side to make a sandwich.

These creamy little bites are always a popular petit four—sweet yet tangy, honeyed, and elegant. Note that for this recipe you will need 1-inch (2.5 cm) dome moulds if you want to make them the way we do at the Inn. However, you can also make this in a larger format—in that case, set the goat cheese mousse first and then pour the gelée on top to set.

BURNT-HONEY GELÉE with GOAT CHEESE MOUSSE

MOUSSE

1½ cups (350 g) fresh, creamy
   goat cheese
⅜ cup (100 mL) cream
3 gelatin sheets, rehydrated, or
   1½ tsp (6 g) powdered gelatin
1 cup (250 mL) whipping cream
Salt and cracked black pepper to
   taste

GELÉE

¼ cup (60 mL) honey
¼ cup (60 mL) apple cider vinegar
2 sheets gelatin, rehydrated, or
   1 tsp (4 g) powdered gelatin

SERVES A CROWD

MAKE THE MOUSSE: In a shallow pot over medium heat, melt the goat cheese with the cream, then add the gelatin, stirring until fully dissolved. Place in a blender or food processor and blend until well mixed, then pour into a bowl and leave to cool to room temperature.

Whip the cream until it achieves firm peaks. Fold the whipped cream into the goat cheese mixture and season to taste with salt and pepper. Set aside, uncovered, at room temperature while you make the gelée.

MAKE THE GELÉE: In a small pot, bring the honey to a boil, cooking it until almost burnt. Deglaze the pot with the apple cider vinegar, then stir in the gelatin. Pour the honey gelée into small silicone dome moulds until half full. Place in the fridge until set, then top with the goat cheese mousse. Chill well until set, then pop out of the dome moulds to serve.

Dramatic, elegant, and delicious, this multi-dimensional dessert is a spectacular way to end an evening. Executive Chef Barr uses tart sea buckthorn berries, which have not only intense flavour but impressive healing properties, and pairs them with sweet, creamy white chocolate. Note that you will need some special equipment for this, including non-stick dehydrator sheets and a whipping siphon (available at bakery supply stores or online), as well as specialized ingredients such as citric acid and agar, a jelly-like substance extracted from algae. Sea buckthorn berries are available frozen in gourmet grocery stores or online.

SEA BUCKTHORN and WHITE CHOCOLATE DESSERT

MAKE THE SEA BUCKTHORN GEL: In a blender, purée the sea buckthorns with the citric acid and water, then pass through a fine-mesh sieve to remove the seeds. Pour the juice into a small saucepan, then use an immersion blender to mix in the agar. Bring to a boil over medium-high heat. Pour into a shallow non-reactive dish, then place in the refrigerator until set, at least 3 hours and preferably overnight. When it has set, dice the gel and purée in a blender until smooth. Keep chilled until ready to use.

MAKE THE SEA BUCKTHORN BUTTER: Prepare an ice bath of water and ice cubes in a large pan. Pour the 1 cup (250 mL) sea buckthorn gel into a large heatproof bowl and set aside.

In a small heatproof bowl set over a pot of simmering water, melt the white chocolate until smooth. In a separate pot over medium heat, warm the oil, clarified butter, glucose, and salt until the mixture reaches 104°F (40°C). Stir the butter mixture into the melted white chocolate. The mixture will split and look very wrong at this point.

Using a hand blender, slowly incorporate the chocolate mixture into the sea buckthorn gel. Place the mixture over the ice bath and continue to mix with the hand blender until well emulsified. Chill in the refrigerator. The mixture may need to be blended again before serving.

Recipe continues ▶

SEA BUCKTHORN GEL
5 cups (675 g) sea buckthorn
   berries
¼ tsp (1 g) citric acid
1 cup (250 mL) water
2 tsp (8 g) agar powder

SEA BUCKTHORN BUTTER
1 cup (250 mL) sea buckthorn gel
13 oz (370 g) white chocolate,
   chopped
¾ cup (185 mL) canola oil
¼ cup (60 mL) clarified butter
¼ cup (60 mL) liquid glucose or
   light corn syrup
Pinch of salt

ALMOND SPONGES
⅞ cup (175 g) sugar
6 eggs
⅓ cup (40 g) flour
1¾ cups (160 g) ground almonds
1 tsp (3 g) salt

CITRUS MERINGUE
3 egg whites
1½ cups (300 g) sugar
⅓ cup (80 mL) water
Finely grated zest of 2 lemons

SEA BUCKTHORN AND LEMON CURD
2¼ cups (220 g) sea buckthorn
   berries
¼ cup (60 mL) lemon juice
⅔ cup (130 g) sugar
4 eggs
1 cup (230 g) butter

ASSEMBLY
Candied orange zest (page 265)
Sea buckthorn sorbet (page 237)

SERVES 6

MAKE THE ALMOND SPONGES: In a food processor, pulse all the ingredients until smooth. Pour into a whipping siphon and charge it twice. Shake well and leave to rest in the fridge for 2 hours. Spray the mixture into small plastic or silicone containers (such as Tupperware) until about 1½ inches (4 cm) thick, then microwave for 1 minute on high. The sponges should be light and not have any wet-looking areas. If any aren't fully cooked, continue to microwave in 15-second increments.

When the sponges are fully baked, leave them to cool in the containers, with the containers flipped upside down. Preheat the oven to 350°F (180°C). Tear the cooled sponges into bite-size pieces and bake in the oven until crispy on the outside but still soft on the inside.

MAKE THE CITRUS MERINGUE: Place the egg whites in the immaculately clean bowl of a stand mixer. In a small pot fitted with a candy thermometer, bring the sugar and water to 239°F (115°C). Immediately start whipping the egg whites on high speed. Bring the sugar mixture to 244°F (118°C), remove from the heat, and slowly pour down the side of the stand-mixer bowl while still whipping on high. Whip until the mixture is cool, then fold in the lemon zest and spread thinly on non-stick dehydrator sheets. Dry until crispy; this will take a few hours or overnight. Break into pieces and store in an airtight container.

MAKE THE SEA BUCKTHORN AND LEMON CURD: In a blender, lightly blend the sea buckthorns and lemon juice, then pass through a fine-mesh strainer to remove the seeds. In a heatproof bowl placed over a double boiler with simmering water, combine the juice, sugar, and eggs and cook until the mixture reaches 183°F (84°C) and is thick enough to coat the back of a spoon. Whisk in the butter until fully incorporated, then transfer to the refrigerator to cool.

TO ASSEMBLE: Place a generous dollop of sea buckthorn butter in the middle of each of six plates. Using an offset spatula, drag the butter across the plates in an appealing fashion. Garnish the butter with dollops of sea buckthorn and lemon curd and pieces of toasted almond sponge and crispy citrus meringue. Finish the dish with candied orange zest and a scoop of sea buckthorn sorbet.

Sabayon—or, in Italy, zabaglione—is a light, slightly boozy custard that is delicious on its own or served with fresh fruit. Chef Filatow's version makes the most of Okanagan Valley fruit, first with the liqueur, then the berry purée in the sabayon, and finally in the serving. "It's fantastic with fresh or canned peaches or strawberries and vanilla ice cream," he says.

Okanagan Spirits RASPBERRY SABAYON

4 egg yolks
¾ cup (150 g) sugar
¼ cup (60 mL) Okanagan Spirits or other raspberry liqueur
½ cup (125 mL) raspberry purée (page 271)
1 cup (250 mL) whipping cream

SERVES 4

Fill a large pot with a couple inches (about 5 cm) of water and bring to a boil.

In a heatproof bowl, whisk together the egg yolks, sugar, liqueur, and raspberry purée, then place over the boiling water and keep whisking until thickened. Remove from the heat and cool to room temperature.

Whip the cream until soft peaks form, then fold into the raspberry mixture. Divide between four bowls or glasses and chill until ready to serve. Serve with additional fresh fruit (like peaches or strawberries) and ice cream or whipped cream.

There's nothing plain vanilla about this rich ice cream by Pastry Chef Conradi.
It makes a luxurious topping for countless desserts, such as the Apple Croustade
(page 212), but is also irresistible enjoyed on its own. Keep it in the freezer and you
can easily add a small scoop to any dessert as needed.

TAHITIAN VANILLA ICE CREAM

4 cups (1 L) milk
Scraped out seeds of 2 Tahitian
    vanilla beans
Finely grated zest of 2 lemons
1¼ cups (250 g) sugar
6 eggs

MAKES ABOUT 4 CUPS
(1 L)

Prepare an ice bath: Fill a large bowl or basin halfway with water and ice cubes.

In a saucepan over medium heat, mix together the milk, vanilla, lemon zest, and about half the sugar and bring slowly to a boil, stirring frequently. This should take 10 to 15 minutes.

In a separate bowl, whisk the eggs with the remaining sugar until light and creamy.

Slowly pour a little hot milk mixture into the eggs, whisking constantly, to temper the eggs. Then carefully whisk the eggs into the pot of hot milk, stirring and cooking to a creamy texture thick enough for the whisk to leave marks. Do not allow the eggs to cook and become grainy—an instant-read thermometer should register between 156°F (70°C) and 185°F (85°C).

Remove from the heat and immediately plunge the pot into the ice bath, stirring constantly, until the custard cools. For best results, cover with plastic wrap pressed right on the surface of the custard (to prevent a tough skin from forming) and refrigerate for a few hours or overnight.

When the custard is chilled, freeze in an ice cream machine according to the manufacturer's instructions. Keep frozen until needed.

In this recipe from Executive Chef Barr, the hay is toasted and infused into milk, which is then transformed into a rich ice cream. The hay adds a nutty, delicately grassy note to the ice cream, enhanced with a touch of cinnamon. Sophisticated yet earthy, this is both dessert and conversation starter.

SPICED-HAY ICE CREAM

Preheat the oven to 250°F (120°C). Spread the hay on a baking sheet and toast for 30 minutes. If you are using a convection oven with a fan, place a second baking sheet on top to prevent the hay from blowing around in the oven. Remove from the oven and place in a large bowl. Add the cinnamon sticks to the toasted hay.

In a pot, bring the milk to a boil, then pour over the toasted hay and cinnamon sticks and transfer to the refrigerator to infuse overnight.

The next day, strain out the hay and cinnamon sticks and, if needed, top up the milk so you have 4 cups (1 L). In a saucepan over low heat, reheat the infused milk, then add the sugar, stabilizer (if using), egg yolks, and cream. Bring to 183°F (84°C) over low heat, stirring frequently to avoid the eggs curdling. Once the mixture has thickened, strain it with a fine-mesh strainer and cool it in a bowl over an ice bath. Refrigerate overnight. The next day, freeze in an ice cream maker according to the manufacturer's instructions.

2 oz (60 g) very clean hay

3 sticks cinnamon

4 cups (1 L) milk, plus additional as needed

¾ cup (150 g) sugar

1 tsp (5 g) ice cream stabilizer, such as carrageenan or guar gum (optional)

15 egg yolks

2 cups (500 mL) whipping cream

MAKES ABOUT 8 CUPS (2 L)

Not just bitter, but sweet, tart, and rich: Pastry Chef Conradi's ice cream is a most sophisticated way to end a meal. You will need an ice cream machine to make this—and the patience to wait until it's frozen so you can enjoy all its layers of flavour.

BITTER CHOCOLATE RASPBERRY ICE CREAM

ICE CREAM BASE

2 cups (500 mL) cream

1 cup (250 mL) 2% milk

1 cup (200 g) sugar

2 eggs

1½ Tbsp (20 g) stabilizer, such as guar gum or carrageenan

½ tsp (2 mL) vanilla extract

BITTER CHOCOLATE RASPBERRY ICE CREAM

⅞ cup (75 g) cocoa powder

¼ cup (50 g) sugar

1 cup (250 mL) milk

1 Tbsp (15 g) butter

1 cup (250 mL) raspberry purée (page 271)

MAKES ABOUT 4 CUPS (1 L)

PREPARE AN ICE BATH: Fill a large bowl or basin halfway with water and ice cubes.

MAKE THE ICE CREAM BASE: In a saucepan over medium heat, mix together the cream, milk, and about half of the sugar and bring slowly to a boil, stirring frequently.

In a separate bowl, whisk the eggs with the remaining sugar until light and creamy.

Slowly pour a little hot milk mixture into the eggs, whisking constantly, to temper the eggs. Then carefully whisk the eggs into the pot of hot milk, stirring and cooking to a creamy texture thick enough for the whisk to leave marks. Do not allow the eggs to cook and become grainy—an instant-read thermometer should register between 156°F (70°C) and 185°F (85°C).

Remove from the heat, whisk in the stabilizer and vanilla extract, and immediately plunge the pot into the ice bath, stirring constantly, until the egg mixture cools.

Refrigerate for 20 minutes, then transfer to an ice cream machine and freeze for 20 minutes before adding flavourings. Do not freeze too long or it will become too firm to add the flavourings.

FINISH THE ICE CREAM: In a saucepan over medium heat, bring the cocoa powder, sugar, milk, and butter to a boil, stirring constantly; be careful, this mixture burns easily.

Plunge the pot into an ice bath to cool the mixture down, then add to the ice cream base in the ice cream machine and freeze according to the manufacturer's instructions.

Scrape the frozen ice cream into a container, a few spoonfuls at a time, interspersing with layers of raspberry purée and gently mixing in the purée to create swirls.

CHOCOLATE ICE CREAM

This simple, classic chocolate ice cream is delicious on its own or alongside treats like the chocolate and hazelnut dessert on page 204.

In a pot, heat the milk until nearly boiling, then add the sugar, stabilizer (if using), and invert sugar or light corn syrup and mix together.

Place the chocolate chunks in a heatproof bowl. Pour the hot milk mixture over the chocolate and whisk until melted and well blended. Strain through a fine-mesh strainer, then cool in a bowl over an ice bath. Refrigerate overnight. The next day, freeze in an ice cream maker according to the manufacturer's instructions.

8 cups (2 L) milk

¾ cup (150 g) sugar

1 Tbsp (15 g) ice cream stabilizer, such as carrageenan or guar gum (optional)

½ cup (125 mL) invert sugar or light corn syrup (see note on page 208)

3 cups (510 g) chopped (small chunks) 64% chocolate

MAKES ABOUT 8 CUPS (2 L)

COCOA NIB DENTELLE

Halfway between cookie and candy, this sweet, crisp, chocolatey bite makes a great garnish for elegant sweets like ice cream or the chocolate hazelnut dessert on page 204.

Preheat the oven to 275°F (135°C). Arrange a silicone liner on a rimmed baking sheet.

Clip a candy thermometer to the side of a medium-size saucepan and place over medium heat. Mix the sugar and pectin in the pot; when well mixed, add the remaining ingredients and cook until the mixture reaches 223°F (106°C).

Spread onto the silicone-lined baking sheet and bake for 2 to 4 minutes. Remove from the oven, cool to room temperature, then break into attractive bite-size pieces. Store in a well-sealed container for up to a week.

SERVES A CROWD

3 cups (600 g) sugar

2 tsp (10 mL) liquid pectin

⅔ cup (145 g) cocoa butter

¼ cup (21 g) cocoa powder

⅔ cup (150 g) butter

½ cup (125 mL) liquid glucose or light corn syrup

1 cup (250 mL) water

STRAWBERRY and ELDERFLOWER SORBET

2.2 lb (1 kg) frozen strawberries

⅔ cup (114 g) glucose powder (also known as dextrose, available in bakery supply stores)

1 Tbsp (11 mL) sorbet stabilizer, such as carrageenan or guar gum (optional)

2 cups (400 g) sugar

1½ Tbsp (30 g) invert sugar or light corn syrup (see note on page 208)

5 cups (1.25 L) elderflower cordial

¼ cup (60 mL) lemon juice

MAKES ABOUT 6 CUPS (1.5 L)

Two of spring's most distinctive flavours, strawberries and frothy white elderflower come together in this cool, refreshing sorbet. The Inn's chefs forage for the fragrant elderflower, which has a delicate aroma like Muscat grapes and white peaches, and make their own cordial. Luckily, you can find it ready-made at gourmet stores.

Thaw the strawberries, place in a blender or food processor, and blend until smooth, then pass through a fine-mesh strainer to remove the seeds. Place the strawberry purée in a saucepan and bring to a boil, then reduce to a simmer.

In a medium-size bowl, whisk together the glucose powder, sorbet stabilizer, and sugar, then stir into the simmering purée. Cook for a minute or two. Add the invert sugar or light corn syrup, cordial, and lemon juice, then pass through a strainer and chill the remaining mixture in a bowl over an ice bath. Once cooled, spin in an ice cream machine and freeze according to the manufacturer's instructions.

OREGON GRAPE SORBET

1½ lb (675 g) Oregon grapes

3 cups (450 g) fresh blueberries

½ cup (100 g) sugar

1 Tbsp (15 mL) honey

1 tsp (5 g) sorbet stabilizer, such as carrageenan or guar gum (optional)

¼ cup (40 g) glucose powder (also known as dextrose, available in bakery supply stores)

MAKES ABOUT 2 CUPS (500 ML)

The Oregon grape is the tiny blue berry of a low-lying evergreen shrub that grows wild all along this coast. First Nations people prized it for its digestive health properties. At the Inn, the chefs prize it for its bright flavour—distinctly grapey, but spicier. If you can't get hold of the real thing, you can use blueberries or Concord grapes instead. If you're using the sweeter Concord grapes, reduce the sugar to ¼ cup (50 g).

Make the Oregon grape juice: In a double boiler, cook the Oregon grapes for 1 hour, then place the contents in a cheesecloth over a bowl and squeeze out the juice. Discard the pulp.

In a food processor or blender, purée the blueberries until smooth. Use a fine-mesh strainer to strain out the pulp and seeds, then set the purée aside.

In a large saucepan, combine 1 cup (250 mL) of the Oregon grape juice and all the other ingredients except the blueberry purée. Bring to a boil, and continue to boil for 5 minutes. Add the purée and whisk to combine. Remove from the heat and chill completely, then freeze in an ice cream machine according to the manufacturer's instructions.

SEA BUCKTHORN SORBET

Sea buckthorn has been getting a lot of attention for its healing properties. This small, golden berry is rich with vitamins, antioxidants, amino acids, and minerals. It is said to improve blood pressure, lower cholesterol, and boost immunity, and it is good for the skin. But at the Inn, Executive Chef Barr loves the berry for its intenly tart, slightly pineapple-like flavour, which simply pops in this refreshing sorbet.

In a blender or food processor, lightly purée the sea buckthorn berries and 1 cup (250 mL) water. Strain through a fine-mesh strainer, removing the seeds and reserving the purée.

In a medium-size pot, bring the remaining 1¼ cups (300 mL) water and the sugar, stabilizer (if using), and invert sugar or light corn syrup to a boil. Whisk in the purée and lemon juice and return to a boil. Remove from the heat and cool completely, then freeze in an ice cream machine according to the manufacturer's directions.

7½ to 8 cups (750 g) sea buck-thorn berries

2¼ cups (550 mL) water

1 cup (200 g) sugar

1 tsp (5 g) sorbet stabilizer, such as carregeenan or guar gum (optional)

1 Tbsp (15 g) invert sugar or light corn syrup (see note on page 208)

⅜ cup (90 mL) lemon juice

MAKES ABOUT 6 CUPS (1.5 L)

*Chef Conradi's favourite dessert was his luxuriously complex chocolate platter:
"basically a little personal chocolate buffet for two people."*

Chef Profile: MATTHIAS CONRADI

MATTHIAS CONRADI REMEMBERS what a hothead he
was when he started at the Inn as a young pastry chef back in 1998. That
may surprise his colleagues, who speak of him as calm and orderly and
exceptionally well organized—all essential attributes for a master of
sugar and chocolate, cakes and tarts. Working at the Wickaninnish Inn
"made me calm down more and improve my patience," he says now.

Chef Conradi joined the Inn from Switzerland, where he was
working at another Relais & Châteaux property. He ended up staying at
the Inn until 2001, then returning from 2004 to 2005. His favourite
memory is of winning the Grand Marnier Dessert Challenge; his
favourite dessert was his luxuriously complex chocolate platter for two.
"It was presented on a black granite slab and was basically a little
personal chocolate buffet for two people," he says.

The Inn is famous as a wedding and elopement destination, and
Chef Conradi delighted in creating gâteaux that were beautiful and
delicious centrepiece to any wedding feast. The most memorable is his
sensational chocolate wedding cake—the gloriously chocolatey three-
layered extravaganza pictured opposite.

Chef Conradi especially loved working with all the berries found
around Tofino, like the cynamokas and salmonberries. Luckily, he's still
got access to those, as he hasn't moved all that far away: today, Chef
Conradi is the chef pâtissier at Villa Eyrie just outside Victoria.

But he still remembers his time at the Wickaninnish fondly. "It is a
great place and company to work for," he says. "I probably would go back
there in a heartbeat if I had the chance."

◀ *Chef Conradi's Chocolate Wedding Cake (recipe not included)*

On the Rocks

▼

WINE CELLAR
AND COCKTAILS

AS GUESTS ENTER The Pointe Restaurant, little do they know that under their feet lies liquid treasure. In the cool, shallow space between the floorboards and the rocks that form the Inn's foundation are cases and cases of wine squirrelled away in a spot that might be inconvenient for the tall, but perfect for keeping wine at exactly the right temperature and humidity.

Wine, spirits, and cocktails are the province of Ike Seaman (pictured opposite), food and beverage director and, since 2013, the Inn's sommelier. Except for a short stint as a fisherman, he's been at the Inn since joining as a server six months after it opened. When Ike returned from his fishing sabbatical, he realized the Inn's wine program needed to mirror the culinary vision of being local, seasonal, and sustainable. "Part of my goal was to rebuild the strength of British Columbia wines included on our list," he says. "Not only to put on the list the best BC wineries, but to put on the list the best wines they produce. I really wanted to bring the wine list in parallel with our food program."

Today, the Inn has about 600 wines on the list and 6,000 bottles in the cellar. Most are from British Columbia, including all the wines by the glass, except for the champagne, which is Taittinger. "We're family-owned, boutique, and sustainable, and search out wineries that reflect our philosophy, such as Blue Mountain Vineyard from Okanagan Falls, a small family-owned winery with an emphasis on quality and sustainability," says Ike. "There are so many amazing wines in the Okanagan and we'd like to showcase them all. The rock and a hard place with a wine list like this is that for many of these wines, only a few cases are available in the province, and once they're gone, they're gone."

Given the Inn's strong focus on wine, members of our evening service team must have a Level 2 certification from the International Sommelier Guild (ISG) or the Wine & Spirit Education Trust (WSET), or an equivalent in-house program. Weekly menu pairings are discussed and tasted to introduce the team to new wines.

For cocktail connoisseurs, the Inn's bartenders shake up an excellent selection of classics and house originals. Many of the cocktails rely on housemade infusions, often made with local ingredients like spruce tips, elderflowers, and huckleberries. Whisky lovers enjoy spending time at the cedar bar in On the Rocks Lounge, which has one of the biggest single-malt selections in western Canada, with more than 100 to choose from.

Ike Seaman, food and beverage director

FEATHER GEORGE

A few drops of mezcal

1½ oz (45 mL) cedar-infused rye whisky (recipe below)

½ oz (15 mL) sweet vermouth, preferably Cinzano Rosso

¼ oz (7 mL) apricot-infused vodka (recipe below)

Cedar curl and orange twist, for garnish (optional)

SERVES 1

Named for artist "Feather George" Yearsley, who can be found at Henry Nolla's carving shed on Chesterman Beach creating his own amazing works. This drink combines the woodsy aromas of cedar with just a whiff of smoke.

Rinse—preferably with a mister—an Old Fashioned glass with a few drops of mezcal. Place the rest of the ingredients except the garnish into a mixing glass and stir with ice. Strain into the prepared Old Fashioned glass, add fresh ice, and, if you like, garnish with a cedar curl and orange twist.

Cedar-Infused Rye Whisky

Cedar, untreated and thoroughly cleaned

1 bottle of rye (preferably J.P. Wiser's)

MAKES 3 CUPS (750 ML)

To make the cedar-infused rye whisky, first make sure any cedar you use is clean and untreated. Cut some kindling-size pieces about ½ inch (1 cm) thick and short enough to fit into a large glass jar, then sterilize them: scrub them well, put them in a pot of water, bring to a boil, and simmer for about 10 minutes. Place them into an immaculately clean glass jar that will hold at least 8 cups (2 L) of liquid.

Pour the bottle of rye overtop, cover, and place in a cool, dark place for up to 1 week, shaking and checking the flavour occasionally. When it's ready, carefully fine-strain out any solids and discard.

Apricot-Infused Vodka

1½ cups (195 g) chopped organic apricots

1 bottle of vodka (preferably Luksusowa)

MAKES 3 CUPS (750 ML)

Clean, chop, and seed enough dried organic apricots to yield about 1½ cups (195 g) fruit. Place the apricots in a large, immaculately clean glass jar. Pour a bottle of vodka over top, shake, seal, and place in a cool, dark place for about a week. Shake it occasionally and taste to see how the flavour is developing. When it's ready, strain out the fruit and discard.

Feather George ▶

GREEN WAVE

¼ cucumber

¼ apple, plus additional for
     garnish

1 sprig mint, plus additional for
     garnish

1½ oz (45 mL) vodka, preferably
     Luksusowa

¾ oz (22 mL) green Chartreuse

¾ oz (22 mL) simple syrup
     (recipe below)

¾ oz (22 mL) lime juice

Fresh and refreshing, just like a spring day when all the new green growth fills the woods around the Inn with vibrant colour.

Peel the cucumber and cut into four ½-inch (1 cm) cubes. Peel the apple and cut into small cubes. Place the cucumbers, apples, and a handful of mint into a cocktail shaker and muddle. Pour in the rest of the ingredients. Add ice and shake well. Fine-strain into an Old Fashioned glass. Add ice. Garnish with a thin slice of apple and mint.

Simple Syrup

1 cup (200g) sugar

**MAKES ABOUT 1¼ CUPS
(300 ML)**

Bring the sugar and 1 cup (250 mL) water just to a boil, stirring constantly until sugar is fully dissolved. Cool to room temperature, then refrigerate until ready to use.

THE 1st GO

When the first warm, sunny day of summer arrives, it's time for that first go on a surfboard. Soon after that, it's time for this refreshing ginger-flavoured cocktail.

In a cocktail shaker or mixing glass, muddle the basil and ginger. Add ice and the rest of the ingredients except the garnish. Stir well and double-strain into a martini glass. If you like, garnish with a piece of candied ginger.

3 basil leaves
2 to 3 coins ginger, peeled
2 oz (60 mL) reposado tequila, such as Hornitos
1 oz (30 mL) lime juice
1 oz (30 mL) ginger syrup (recipe below)
Candied ginger, for garnish (optional)

SERVES 1

Ginger Syrup

If you can't find commercially produced ginger syrup, you can make your own by adding the ginger and sugar to 1 cup (250 mL) water in a pot. Bring the mixture to a boil, stirring constantly, until the sugar is fully dissolved. Remove from the heat and let it steep for at least 30 minutes, then strain out the ginger.

Handful peeled, chopped ginger
1 cup (200 g) sugar

MAKES ABOUT 1¼ CUPS (200 ML)

ESPRESSO MARTINI

When the nights are chilly at the Inn, there's nothing like curling up in front of the fire with this rich, creamy, coffee-flavoured cocktail.

Place all the ingredients except the garnish in a shaker with ice. Shake well. Strain into a chilled martini glass. If you like, garnish with coffee beans.

1 oz (30 mL) espresso, cooled, such as Caffè Umbria Gusto Crema
1 oz (30 mL) Sheringham chocolate vodka
½ oz (15 mL) Baileys Irish Cream
½ oz (15 mL) Kahlúa coffee liqueur
1 oz (30 mL) whipping cream
3 coffee beans, for garnish (optional)

SERVES 1

As the days get colder and shorter, we crave deeper, richer, heartier flavours. This cocktail, made with the huckleberries that grow all around the Inn, serves those cravings beautifully. The Inn uses locally made Stump Coastal Forest Gin from Phillips Fermentorium Distilling Co. in Victoria.

FORAGING through the WOODS

1 pear
1 oz (30 mL) cane syrup
1 oz (30 mL) lemon juice
1 oz (30 mL) huckleberry liqueur
    (recipe below)
1 oz (30 mL) gin, preferably
    locally made
Dehydrated pear chip, for garnish
    (optional)

SERVES 1

Peel, core, and chop the pear. Place in a cocktail shaker along with the cane syrup and lemon juice and muddle. Add the remaining ingredients except the garnish and shake well. Fine-strain into a martini glass. If you like, garnish with a dehydrated pear chip.

Huckleberry Liqueur

4 cups (592 g) huckleberries,
    thoroughly cleaned
1 bottle of vodka
1½ cups (300 g) sugar

**MAKES ABOUT 8 CUPS
(2 L)**

Place about 4 cups (592 g) well-cleaned huckleberries in a sterilized glass jar that can hold at least 8 cups (2 L) of liquid. (If you can't find huckleberries, you can use blackberries or raspberries instead.) Mash them well, then add a bottle of vodka to the jar, stirring to combine. Cover and place in a cool, dark place for 2 weeks. Shake or stir every couple of days. Fine-strain out any solids, wash out the jar, and return the infusion to the jar. Create a simple syrup with 1½ cups (375 mL) water and the sugar and add to the infusion, stirring well. Age 2 more weeks, then fine-strain through cheesecloth.

Chef Wilson's sourdough breads—flavoured with herbs, rich with cheese—were the stuff of legend. Guests would order extra.

Chef Profile: **MATT WILSON**

MATT WILSON IS originally from Australia, where he worked at luxury establishments such as the Peppers Manor House in New South Wales. He left Australia to move to England, where he worked at the Bath Priory Hotel, a MichelZin-starred property. He came to Canada in 2007 and started at Vancouver's acclaimed Nu restaurant, before continuing west to Tofino a year later to join the Inn as pastry chef.

During his time at the Inn, Chef Wilson brought forward major changes to the culinary program. He created innovative desserts that raised the bar—not only with quality ingredients, but unconventional ones as well, such as west coast cedar, popcorn, yuzu, and black tea. Very memorably, he also explored the myriad ways to make bread. Every day, he'd create four different house-baked loaves. His sourdough-based breads, which were flavoured with herbs, rich with cheese, or perhaps studded with his favourite local ingredients—cedar, salal berries, and chanterelle mushrooms—were the stuff of legend. Visitors would swing by just to pick up a loaf. Guests would order extra.

Working at the Wickaninnish Inn, Chef Wilson says, "gave me the chance to grow as a chef and determine my own style." He moved on in 2013, and for a number of years was the Executive Pastry Chef at Michael Noble's The Nash and Off Cut Bar in Calgary. More recently, he joined Hudson, the private dining space attached to Oliver & Bonacini's The Guild restaurant, as chef de cuisine. There, in one of Calgary's most glamorous heritage buildings, his talent for culinary innovation and unconventional ingredients continues to shine.

◀ *Chef Wilson's Tuff Session Sourdough Bread (recipe on page 71)*

The Pantry

▼

VINEGARS, OILS, PRESERVES, AND MORE

The pantry at the Wickaninnish Inn is an Aladdin's cave of glorious flavours and textures.

THE LAND AND SEA surrounding the Inn may be nature's grocery store, but it's not exactly the kind of supermarket that carries everything a cook could want at all times. Ingredients come into season, and then they're gone. The only way to capture their evanescent flavours is to preserve them. Berries thicken into jams, flowers infuse vinegars, herbs bring life to oils. Preserving fresh ingredients transforms them into products with depth and life and multiple uses. More than that, though, it allows a chef or home cook to add their own signature touch to every single dish they make. What, after all, could be more personal than your own handcrafted mustard or spiced oil?

And so the pantry at the Wickaninnish Inn is an Aladdin's cave of glorious flavours and textures, at once a practical necessity and a joyful culinary destination, the tastes of the region captured in a jar or bottle.

For the home cook, these are the ingredients that will elevate your dishes to a whole new level. More than that, they will bring the Inn into your home, captured in a drop of spiced oil or a spoonful of marmalade. Stock up on these and you will have a houseful of handy flavours always at your disposal.

Vinegars preserve delicate florals or the briny taste of seaweed and add vibrant life to salads and sauces. Vinegars can keep, refrigerated, for up to six months.

VINEGARS

Elderflower Vinegar

2 cups (500 mL) water
2 Tbsp (30 mL) honey
2 cups (500 mL) white balsamic
    vinegar
Juice of ½ lemon
3 large elderflowers

MAKES 4 CUPS (1 L)

Heat the water and honey just until the honey dissolves. Combine with the vinegar and lemon juice and cool to room temperature. Place the elderflowers in a clean glass container, such as a large mason jar, and cover with the vinegar mixture. Steep in the fridge overnight, then strain the flowers from the liquid. Pour the vinegar into a sterilized glass bottle and keep refrigerated.

Kelp Vinegar

2 cups (500 mL) white wine
    vinegar
2 cups (500 mL) water
3 Tbsp (30 g) powdered dried bull
    kelp, available online or at
    specialty markets

MAKES 4 CUPS (1 L)

Combine all the ingredients in a blender, then place in a clean glass jar in the fridge for 3 days. Strain through a coffee filter and pour the vinegar into a sterilized glass bottle. Keep refrigerated.

Flavoured oils capture the pungency of spices and herbs, adding layers of zing to a variety of dishes. It's best to keep oils refrigerated to avoid spoilage; bring them to room temperature when ready to use. They should last about a month.

FLAVOURED OILS

Leek Oil

In a blender or food processor, purée the oil and leek tops well. Pour into a plastic container and freeze overnight.

The next day, remove the frozen oil from the plastic container, hang it in a muslin bag, and allow it to thaw—place a freezer-safe pan under the bag to catch the liquid, squeezing the bag to extract as much liquid and colour as you can. Discard the pulp.

Freeze the oil overnight. The green leek oil will rise to the top. The next day, pour the oil into a jar and discard the frozen water at the bottom of the pan. Pour the oil into a clean, airtight glass container. Must be kept refrigerated.

2 cups (500 mL) grapeseed oil
2 leeks, green part only, washed and chopped

MAKES ABOUT 2 CUPS (500 ML)

Cumin Oil

In a blender or food processor, combine all the ingredients and purée. Pour the contents of the blender into a pot and heat over medium just to a simmer. Remove from the heat and steep overnight, covered. Heat again over medium heat, then strain through a filter cone, cheesecloth, or fine-mesh strainer. Pour the oil into a clean, airtight glass container. Must be kept refrigerated.

¼ cup (24 g) ground cumin
½ red bell pepper
1 tsp (2 g) paprika
½ tsp (1 g) cayenne pepper
2 cloves garlic, sliced
Peel of ¼ orange
Peel of ¼ lemon
2½ cups (625 mL) canola oil

MAKES ABOUT 2 CUPS (500 ML)

259

Curry Oil

1 onion, chopped

3 stalks celery, chopped

6 cloves garlic, sliced

2 apples, diced

¼ lb (110 g) ginger, peeled and cut into chunks

Finely grated zest of 2 lemons

Finely grated zest of 2 limes

4 pods star anise

2 Tbsp (10 g) coriander seeds

2 Tbsp (10 g) cumin seeds

2 Tbsp (10 g) mustard seeds

¼ cup (15 g) chopped cilantro leaves

1½ cups (145 g) curry powder

2 Tbsp (30 mL) tomato paste

6 cups (1.5 L) vegetable oil

MAKES ABOUT 6 CUPS (1.5 L)

Combine all the ingredients, except the oil, in a pot. Cover with the oil and bring to a simmer over medium heat for 5 minutes. Remove from the heat and let the oil steep overnight. The next day, strain through cheesecloth. Pour the oil into a clean, airtight glass container. Must be kept refrigerated.

Dill Oil

2 cups (500 mL) grapeseed oil

3 bunches dill, roughly chopped

4 sprigs flat-leaf parsley, leaves only

MAKES ABOUT 2 CUPS (500 ML)

In a blender, combine the ingredients and run on high speed until the blender jug is slightly warm to the touch. Strain the oil through a coffee filter into a bowl set in an ice bath to cool down. Transfer the oil to a plastic container and place in the freezer overnight. The next day, pour the oil off into a very clean, airtight glass container, leaving the frozen water at the bottom of the plastic container. Oil must be kept refrigerated.

Hemlock Oil

In a small pot, heat the hemlock tips and oil to 150°F (65°C) and hold there for 45 minutes. Cool the oil and tips to room temperature, then place in a blender with the parsley. Purée on high speed until the jug is warm to the touch. Strain the oil through a filter cone or cheesecloth into a bowl set in an ice bath. Transfer the oil to a plastic container and place in the freezer overnight. The next day, pour the oil off into a very clean, airtight glass container, leaving the frozen water at the bottom of the plastic container. Oil must be kept refrigerated.

Note that the same recipe can be made with spruce tips instead of hemlock.

¼ lb (125 g) tender young hemlock tips (the bright green new growth; see note)

2 cups (500 mL) grapeseed oil

2 bunches flat-leaf parsley, leaves only

MAKES ABOUT 2 CUPS (500 ML)

HEMLOCK

The western hemlock is not the poisonous weed known for taking the life of the ancient Greek philosopher Socrates, but a coastal conifer that has edible components and has been enjoyed for millennia by local First Nations. It has a delicate, slightly citrusy flavour. The Inn's chefs use it in a variety of dishes and condiments, including salt, vinegar, oil, and pickles.

Chef Filatow's housemade mustard adds a personal touch to the quintessential condiment, especially with the addition of fresh herbs, and is a perfect accompaniment to sandwiches, burgers, and charcuterie. Mustards that have been processed in a hot water bath will last up to a year, unopened, in the pantry; refrigerate after opening.

MUSTARDS

Grainy Mustard

Place the mustard seeds in a 4-cup (1 L) glass jar. Pour in enough vinegar to cover the seeds, then cover with a lid.

Let the mixture sit at room temperature for 2 weeks. Check every other day to make sure the vinegar is always covering the seeds. Top up as necessary.

Once the seeds are soft and most of the bitterness has gone, it's time to finish the mustard. Strain the mustard from the vinegar. Set the liquid aside for later use.

In a blender or food processor, pulse the seeds to break up some of them. Purée until the desired consistency is reached, adding the reserved vinegar as needed. Add the honey and salt to taste.

Scrape into very clean jars and, if you like, process in a hot-water bath. (See The Preserving Process on page 247.) Use as you would any other grainy mustard.

⅔ cup (130 g) yellow mustard seeds

⅔ cup (130 g) black or red mustard seeds

1½ cups (375 mL) apple cider vinegar, plus additional if needed

1 tsp (5 mL) honey

Sea salt to taste

MAKES ABOUT 2 CUPS (500 ML)

VARIATIONS

Tarragon mustard: For a quintessentially French mustard, use white wine vinegar instead of cider vinegar and add a couple of sprigs of tarragon to the mustard seeds as they soak.

Brown mustard: Use malt vinegar instead of cider vinegar and brown sugar instead of honey for a mustard that would be delicious with sausages.

Verjus Mustard

1⅓ cups (260 g) yellow mustard seeds

⅔ cup (85 g) golden raisins

1½ cups (375 mL) verjus (a tangy grape juice, not quite vinegar)

1 tsp (2 g) ground allspice

⅜ cup (100 mL) champagne vinegar

2 Tbsp (30 mL) honey

2 cups (500 mL) water

MAKES ABOUT 1½ CUPS (375 ML)

Soak the mustard seeds in water for 48 hours, then rinse well under running water to remove the slippery residue. Soak the raisins overnight in the verjus. In a small pot, combine all the ingredients and simmer for 1 hour, until the liquid has reduced by two-thirds. Place in a food processor and blend until the mustard comes together as a cohesive spread. Store refrigerated in a very clean glass jar.

Pickles extend the all-too-short lifespan of seasonal ingredients like spruce tips, seaweed, or wild mushrooms.

PICKLES

Pickled Hemlock Tips

¼ lb (110 g) tender young hemlock tips (the bright green new growth; see note on page 243)

2 Tbsp (30 mL) honey

1¼ cups (300 mL) water

1 cup (250 mL) white wine vinegar

1 tsp (3 g) salt

MAKES ABOUT 2 CUPS (500 ML)

Rinse the hemlock tips carefully. Sterilize a 4-cup (1 L) glass jar and place the hemlock tips in the jar. Note that you can also use spruce tips if hemlock is unavailable.

In a small pot over medium-high heat, stir the honey and water together and cook until fully blended. Add the vinegar and salt and continue cooking until salt is dissolved.

Pour the hot vinegar mixture over the hemlock tips in the jar. Let cool to room temperature, then cover and refrigerate. Consume within 2 weeks.

Candying nuts, citrus zest, or other garnishes gives them an appealing caramelized flavour and satisfying crunch. With sugar, heat, and just a touch of salt, it's an easy way to add powerful impact to salads, desserts, and other dishes. Refrigerated, candied garnishes will keep for several months.

CANDIED GARNISHES

Candied Orange Zest

Remove the peels from the oranges in quarters. Scrape off as much of the white pith as you can, then cut the peels into fine strips. Place the orange zest into a small pot, add enough water to cover, and bring to a boil. Strain. Repeat this step three times; this removes some of the bitterness and softens the peels.

In a large non-reactive pot, make a simple syrup by bringing the water and sugar to a boil, stirring until the sugar has completely dissolved. Add the zest and boil until the syrup reduces by half and the zest is translucent, about 15 minutes. Strain off the remaining syrup and toss the candied zest in sugar to coat.

7 oranges
1 cup (250 mL) water, plus additional to boil the zest
1 cup (200 g) sugar, plus additional to coat the zest

MAKES ABOUT 2 CUPS (500 ML)

Candied Hazelnuts

Make a simple syrup: In a medium-size saucepan, bring the sugar and water just to a boil, stirring constantly, until the sugar is fully dissolved.

Using a towel, remove as much of the hazelnuts' skin as you can, then add the nuts to the simple syrup. Bring back up to a boil and cook for 10 minutes.

Strain off the simple syrup (you can reserve the hazelnut-flavoured syrup for another use). Pour the canola oil into a large pot and clip a frying thermometer to the side. Heat the oil to 300°F (150°C), then fry the nuts until well caramelized. Strain off the oil and spread the nuts out on parchment paper to cool. Season with a touch of salt while still a bit sticky. Wait until completely dry before storing in the refrigerator.

4 cups (800 g) sugar
4 cups (1 L) water
1½ cups (215 g) hazelnuts, toasted
4 cups (1 L) canola oil
Salt to taste

MAKES ABOUT 1⅓ CUPS (187 G)

Candied Lichen

2½ cups (500 g) sugar

2 cups (500 mL) water

2 cups (500 mL) reindeer lichen,
  picked clean (see note)

Drizzle of hazelnut oil

Salt to taste

A few toasted hazelnuts,
  microplaned

**MAKES ABOUT 2 CUPS
(500 ML)**

In a large pot, bring the sugar and water to a boil, then cool to room temperature to create a syrup. Wash and dry the reindeer lichen. Soak the lichen in the syrup for 2 hours. Drain the lichen well, place in a dehydrator set at the low temperature, and leave to dry overnight. Once the lichen is crispy, dress with hazelnut oil and salt and finish with toasted hazelnuts.

LICHEN

Lichen is actually two organisms functioning as a single, symbiotic unit: a fungus living with an algae. There are about 17,000 species of lichen worldwide, and many of them are not only edible but, properly prepared, delicious. Lichens have become especially popular in Nordic cuisine, which emphasizes indigenous foraged fare. Among the edible lichens is so-called reindeer lichen, also known as reindeer or caribou moss. (It is an important food source for both, hence the name.) It grows widely around the Inn and has a delicately astringent flavour.

Candied Pecans

¼ cup (60 mL) maple syrup

¼ cup (50 g) sugar

4 cups (570 g) pecans

Salt

MAKES 4 CUPS (568 G)

Preheat the oven to 350°F (180°C). Line a baking sheet with a silicone liner, parchment paper, or non-stick foil.

In a skillet over medium heat, bring the maple syrup and sugar up to a simmer, stirring until the sugar is dissolved. Add the pecans and cook for a couple of minutes, stirring frequently, until the nuts are coated.

Scrape onto the prepared baking sheet, keeping the nuts in a single layer and leaving as much space between them as possible.

Place in the oven and bake for 10 minutes, keeping a watchful eye on the nuts to make sure they don't burn. Remove from the oven and break up any clusters. Sprinkle with salt and allow to cool to room temperature.

Jams, jellies, and marmalades conserve the summery essence of berries and tree fruits, making them available year-round for scones or toast or, when they're this good, eaten straight out of the jar.

PRESERVES

The Preserving Process

Canning is easy and fun to do, but home cooks need to take careful steps to keep everything food-safe. It's essential to have the right tools—including a canning pot, glass jars, unused snap lids and bands, a lifter, a magnetic wand, a funnel, and a ladle—and to follow the procedures below.

STERILIZE THE JARS: Fill a canning pot with enough water to cover the jars by at least 2 inches (5 cm). Place the jars and snap lids in the pot, bring to a boil, and sterilize the jars for at least 10 minutes. Keep them in the pot until just before you're ready to fill the jars; keep the water at a high simmer, as you'll need it to process the filled jars.

FILL THE JARS: When you're ready to fill the jars, remove the jars and snap lids from the canning pot and drain out any water. A jar lifter and magnetic wand are helpful tools for this. Bring the water in the canning pot back up to a boil, adding more water if necessary.

Ladle the hot preserves into the hot jars, leaving about ¼ inch (6 mm) head space and making sure there are no air bubbles in the jars. Keep the rims clean (a wide funnel will help) and wipe up anything that splashes on them. Cover with the snap lids, then screw the bands on finger-tight.

PROCESS THE JARS: Put the filled jars back into the boiling water and process for 10 to 15 minutes. Note that some preserves may need more processing time; check the recipe you're using. Also note that you will need to add more processing time for higher elevations—an additional five minutes for 1,000 to 3,000 feet (305 to 914 metres) above sea level, and 10 minutes for 3,000 to 6,000 feet (914 to 1,829 metres) above sea level. Remove from the water and wait for the snap lids to seal. This will be indicated by a distinct "pop." If you don't hear a pop and there is a small bump on top of the snap lid, the jars have not sealed properly. Keep these ones in the refrigerator and consume their contents within a couple of weeks.

Raspberry Jam

4 cups (492 g) fresh or 4 cups
  (560 g) frozen raspberries
  (thawed if frozen)
7 cups (1.4 kg) sugar
1 package liquid pectin, such as
  Certo
¼ cup (60 mL) lemon juice

**MAKES 4 (8 OZ/250 ML)
JARS**

In a large non-reactive pot over high heat, place the berries and sugar and bring to a boil. Reduce the heat to medium and continue to cook for 15 minutes. Add the pectin and lemon juice, stirring well to combine. Remove from the heat and skim the foam off the surface. Ladle into sterilized jars and either store in the refrigerator or follow the preserving process on page 247.

Strawberry Jam

8 cups (1.2 kg) fresh or 8 cups
  (1.8 kg) frozen strawberries,
  hulled (thawed if frozen)
6 cups (1.2 kg) sugar
2 packages liquid pectin, such as
  Certo
⅓ cup (80 mL) lemon juice

**MAKES 5 TO 6
(8 OZ/250 ML) JARS**

Crush the strawberries roughly with a potato masher so there are no whole berries remaining. Place in a large non-reactive pot, stir in the sugar, and bring to a hard boil. Reduce the heat and simmer for 15 minutes, stirring occasionally. Pour in the pectin and lemon juice and stir well to combine. Remove from the heat and skim the foam off the surface. Ladle into sterilized jars and either store in the refrigerator or follow the preserving process on page 247.

Marmalade

3 oranges
2 lemons
6 cups (1.5 L) water
½ tsp (2 g) baking soda
5½ cups (1.1 kg) sugar
2 packages liquid pectin, such as
  Certo
¼ cup (60 mL) lemon juice

**MAKES 5 TO 6
(8 OZ/250 ML) JARS**

Remove the peels, in quarters, from the oranges and lemons, reserving the fruit. Flatten the peels, then scrape off and discard about half the white pith. Cut the peels into thin slices, then place them in a large saucepan and add the water and baking soda. Stir well. Cover and simmer on low heat for 20 minutes, stirring occasionally.

Chop the peeled fruit and add, with their juices, to the saucepan. Simmer, covered, for 10 minutes. Add the sugar to the fruit and bring to a boil. Boil hard for 30 minutes, stirring occasionally. Add the pectin and lemon juice and stir well to combine. Remove from the heat and skim the foam off the surface. Ladle into sterilized jars and either store in the refrigerator or follow the preserving process on page 247.

Raspberry Purée

In a medium pot over medium heat, bring the raspberries and honey to a boil. Turn down the heat and continue cooking until the liquid is reduced to a thick, syrupy consistency. Purée in a blender or food processor, then pass through a fine-mesh strainer. Cool down on ice. Will keep in the fridge for a couple of days, or in the freezer for up to six months.

2 lb (900 g) frozen raspberries
½ cup (125 mL) honey

MAKES ABOUT 2 CUPS (500 ML)

Apple Butter

Peel and core the apples. Place them in a pot with the apple juice and bring to a boil. Simmer for 30 to 45 minutes or until they are very tender. Place them in a blender or food processor and purée. Pass the purée through a fine-mesh strainer to remove the seeds, reserving the pulp and the juice.

Return the pulp and juice to the pot, add the sugar, lemon juice, and spices, and cook over low heat for about 2 hours or until very thick and deep in colour. Remove from the pot and reserve in the fridge. Alternatively, you can ladle into sterilized jars and follow the preserving process on page 247.

4 lb (1.8 kg) apples, preferably Gala
4 cups (1 L) apple juice
2 cups (400 g) sugar
2 Tbsp (30 mL) lemon juice
1½ tsp (3 g) ground cinnamon
½ tsp (1 g) ground allspice
¼ tsp (0.5 g) ground cloves

MAKES 5 TO 6 CUPS (1.25 TO 1.5 L)

Traditional and not-so-traditional preserving techniques are a key component of contemporary cuisine. Think gels, ashes, pearls, and more. These are the chef's secret arsenal; why not make them yours too? There's no better way to capture the essence of the Wickaninnish Inn and the wild west coast of Vancouver Island, forever to be found in your pantry.

THE REST

Rendered Duck Fat

2 whole ducks
½ cup (125 mL) water

MAKES ABOUT 1 CUP (250 ML)

Carefully remove the duck legs and breasts and set aside (these can be used for confit duck legs, page 256, and cinnamon-scented duck, page 156). Trim all the fat and skin remaining on the birds—you should have about 1 lb (450 g). Reserve the bones to make duck stock (recipe below).

In a small pot over low heat, place the fat, skin, and water and simmer until the fat is rendered, the water evaporates, and the skin has crisped into cracklings. This should take several hours; do not allow it to boil or it will take on a bitter taste. Strain the cracklings from the fat. You should have about 1 cup (250 mL) of duck fat when you're done. Place fat in an immaculately clean jar and cover; it will keep in the refrigerator for several months.

Duck Stock

2 duck carcasses
1 large onion, peeled and
    quartered
2 large carrots, halved crosswise
2 large stalks celery, halved
    crosswise
1 Tbsp (10 g) black peppercorns
1 Tbsp (5 g) whole cloves
3 bay leaves

MAKES 8 TO 12 CUPS (2 TO 3 L)

Place all the ingredients in a stockpot and add enough water to cover by a couple of inches, at least 12 cups (3 L).

Bring to a simmer and continue to cook, uncovered, for 2 to 3 hours, skimming off any grey foam. Do not allow to come to a rolling boil, or the stock will be cloudy. If it seems to be getting dry, add more water.

Strain all the solids using a chinois or large sieve. Place the liquid stock into freezer-safe containers and freeze until you're ready to use.

Confit Duck Legs

Cure the duck: Mix the salt and sugar together and rub all over the duck legs. Place in a non-reactive container, then sprinkle with the thyme, bay leaves, shallots, orange peels, and a few grinds of pepper. Cover with plastic wrap and place in the fridge overnight and up to 48 hours.

Preheat the oven to 180°F (85°C). Rinse the cure off the duck legs, pat them dry, then place them into a small pan or baking dish—they should fit snugly so you need less duck fat to cover them. Melt the duck fat and pour it over the duck legs, making sure they are completely covered, then place in the oven and bake until the meat is falling-off-the-bone tender, at least 6 hours. Store the legs in their own fat; they will last a couple of weeks at least.

3 Tbsp (25 g) salt
1 Tbsp (10 g) sugar
4 duck legs
4 sprigs thyme
2 bay leaves, torn onto pieces
4 shallots, thinly sliced
Peel of 1 orange, sliced
Cracked black pepper to taste
2 cups (500 mL) duck fat, or as needed (page 255)

MAKES 4 CONFIT DUCK LEGS

Cured Egg Yolks

Combine the salt and sugar. On a small plate, make a bed with half of the salt and sugar mix. Make two small indentations and place a yolk in each one, then cover with the remaining salt. Leave uncovered at room temperature for 2 days. The yolks should turn hard and translucent.

Wash off all of the salt and sugar and leave the yolks on parchment paper, uncovered, for 2 weeks at room temperature. The yolks should be very hard and bright yellow at this point and can be grated as a garnish for a variety of dishes.

1 cup (145 g) salt
1 cup (200 g) sugar
2 egg yolks

MAKES 2 EGG YOLKS

2 ice cubes

3 cloves garlic, crushed

1 cup (100 g) grated pecorino
  romano cheese

1 cup (250 mL) canola oil

3 bunches basil, leaves only

Finely grated zest of 1 lemon

⅜ cup (55 g) pumpkin seeds,
  toasted

Salt and cracked black pepper to
  taste

**MAKES ABOUT 2 CUPS
(500 ML)**

Pesto

In a blender or food processor, combine the ice cubes, garlic, cheese, and canola oil. Blend until smooth, then add the basil, lemon zest, and pumpkin seeds. Blend until smooth, then season with salt and pepper. Use right away, or freeze for up to 1 month.

1 Tbsp (5 g) fennel seeds

3 egg yolks, room temperature

1 Tbsp (15 mL) Dijon mustard

1 Tbsp (15 mL) lemon juice

1 Tbsp (15 mL) white wine vinegar

½ cup (125 mL) grapeseed oil

¼ cup (60 mL) olive oil

4 dashes Worcestershire sauce

Sea salt and cracked black pepper
  to taste

**MAKES ABOUT 1 CUP
(250 ML)**

Fennel Mayonnaise

In a skillet over medium heat, lightly toast the fennel seeds, stirring frequently to ensure they don't burn. Allow them to cool, then grind to a fine powder.

In a large mixing bowl or the bowl of a food processor, place the egg yolks, mustard, lemon juice, and vinegar and whisk or process until combined.

Slowly pour the oils in a steady stream into the yolk mixture while whisking or processing continuously and vigorously until the mixture thickens. Once all of the oil is incorporated, add the Worcestershire and ground fennel and season to taste with salt and pepper.

Transfer the mayonnaise to a clean, non-reactive container with a lid and refrigerate until ready to use. This will keep for 2 to 3 weeks in the refrigerator.

Crème Fraîche

Combine the cream and buttermilk and leave at room temperature for 48 hours or until thickened and tangy. Refrigerate until needed. The crème fraîche will keep, covered and chilled, for up to a week.

2 cups (500 mL) cream
1 cup (250 mL) buttermilk

MAKES ABOUT 3 CUPS (750 ML)

Smoked Almond Cream

Light a charcoal smoker or prepare a handheld smoker if you have access to one. Arrange the almonds on a tray and smoke them for 20 minutes. Place the milk in a blender with a pinch of salt. With the blender running, drop in the almonds a few at a time until you have a thick and smooth purée. Pass through a strainer and reserve, covered, in the fridge for up to three days.

1 cup (140 g) peeled almonds
2 cups (500 mL) milk
Pinch of salt

MAKES ABOUT 2 CUPS (500 ML)

Hemlock Salt

Using a mortar and pestle, grind the hemlock tips and salt together or process in a food processor. Place on a tray, and dry, uncovered, at room temperature. It should take about 48 hours until the mixture is completely dry. Grind again into a fine powder, then place in a lidded container and store at room temperature. This makes a great seasoning for celeriac bark (page 148) or even a gourmet bowl of popcorn.

2 oz (60 g) hemlock tips (see note on page 243)
2 Tbsp (20 g) salt

MAKES ABOUT ⅓ CUP (75 G)

Beet Powder

Peel the beets, then slice them very thinly or, better yet, use a mandoline to shave them into paper-thin wafers. Dry them in a dehydrator or on very low temperature in a convection oven. When they are very dry and brittle, cool them to room temperature, then blitz them in a food processor or blender until powdered. Store in the refrigerator for up to two weeks.

2 medium-size red beets

MAKES ABOUT 1 CUP (96 G)

*A 20th anniversary gathering of the Inn's
chefs with Tim Curley, longtime member of
the Inn's culinary team (from left to right:
Warren Barr, Justin Labossiere, Rod Butters,
Tim Curley, Matt Wilson, Matthias Conradi,
Duncan Ly, and Mark Filatow.)*

Acknowledgements

BY CHARLES McDIARMID

I have dreamed for some time about putting together a book like this to celebrate the incredible culinary talents of the Wickaninnish Inn over the past 20 plus years, but I never quite knew where to start. This book would not have been possible without the vision of Joanne Sasvari and her energetic efforts in wrangling chefs, testing recipes, and weaving our stories throughout these pages.

It was amazing, and humbling, to see how quickly and enthusiastically our past chefs came on board, including opening chef Rod Butters, along with Mark Filatow, Andrew Springett, Justin Labossiere, Duncan Ly, Matthias Conradi, and Matt Wilson, who all not only wrote and shared their favourite recipes, but devoted countless hours to the photo shoots to capture their creations. I have the greatest respect and admiration for these chefs, and they will always be a part of our Inn family.

A very special thank you to our Executive Chef Warren Barr, who provided the bulk of the recipes for this book. This was no small ask, and included extra testing, extra photo shoots, and extra editing, all while he was also maintaining our world-class culinary program.

Thank you to Robert McCullough of Appetite for believing in our cookbook project; to Lindsay Paterson who walked us through the process; to Scott Richardson for his beautiful design; and to everyone else at Penguin Random House Canada who helped make this book a reality. Makito Inomata brought our ideas to visual form with his innovative and captivating photography, and was a true pleasure to work with. Claire Macdonald, thank you for your tireless efforts in keeping this project on track and making it happen despite your general fear of kitchens.

Finally, I would like to thank my family, and especially my parents, Howard and Lynn. We often gathered around the table at our family cabin. My mother would prepare wonderful meals, while my father talked to guests about the idea of opening the Wickaninnish Inn. They often thought our plan to build a luxurious property in such a remote location was a little "out to lunch," but I am convinced the great food and lively company around that table helped convince many of our early partners to join us and make the Inn the reality it is today.

◀ *Handcrafted wooden feathers by "Feather" George Yearsley*

Index

condiments. *See* dips and spreads; mustard(s); oil(s); preserve(s); sauce(s); vinegar(s)

confit, orange segment, 170

confit duck legs, 274

Conradi, Matthias, 32, 34–37, 42, 198, 200, 201, 212, 230, 232, **239**

corn
  and clam chowder, 64
  in fish fritters, 106

cornbread, 70

cornmeal
  in cornbread, 70
  in fried polenta, 103

crab
  cakes, 111–12
  cappuccino, 66
  Dungeness, and mascarpone ravioli in saffron pasta, 144–45
  legs, in potlatch, 126–27

crackers, buttermilk, 104

crackers, elk, 163

cranberries
  in ancient grain porridge, 30
  in granola bars, 50

cream
  Chantilly, 48, 217
  in crème fraîche, 276
  cultured, 132

cream cheese
  in apple carrot sour cream muffins, 32
  in fried polenta, 103
  in smoked salmon macarons, 135–36

crème fraîche
  recipe for, 275
  in squash blossoms stuffed with spot prawns, 146

crème pâtissière filling for Danish pastry, 36

cress, wild. *See also* watercress
  in elk with forest flavours, 160–62

crispy pork belly and scallops, 164–66

croustade, apple, 212

cucumbers
  in Green Wave (cocktail), 248
  in salmon mosaic, 132
  in sidestripe shrimp escabeche, 148

cultured cream, 132

cumin aioli, 130

cumin oil, 259

curd, lemon, 210

curd, sea buckthorn and lemon, 226

cured egg yolks, 273

curing salt, about, 177

currant(s). *See also* raisins
  gel, 163
  scones, 40

curried carrot salad, 90–91

curry granola, 90

curry oil, 260

curry paste
  in coconut green curry mussels, 116
  in kuri squash and seafood chowder, 60

curry vinaigrette, 90

cynamoka berry(ies)
  in elk with forest flavours, 160–62
  gel, 163

D

dacquoise, hazelnut, 204

daikon. *See also* radishes
  in salmon mosaic, 132

Danish pastry, 34–37

dates, in granola bars, 50

dentelle, cocoa nib, 233

dill oil, 260

dips and spreads. *See also* mustard(s); preserve(s); sauce(s)
  cumin aioli, 130
  cynamoka berry gel, 163
  fennel mayonnaise, 274
  kale tapenade, 95
  salsa verde, 112
  spicy aioli, 103

double-chocolate mashed-potato brioche, 206

dressings and vinaigrettes

Asian dressing, 128

citrus-mint vinaigrette, 86

curry vinaigrette, 90

lemon dressing, 191

miso dressing, 88

mustard dressing, 178

walnut and verjus dressing, 85

dried fruit granola, 28

duck
  breast, cinnamon-scented, 168–70
  confit potato press, 171
  legs, confit, 273
  rendered fat, 272
  stock, 272

Dungeness crab and mascarpone ravioli in saffron pasta, 144–45

E

egg(s)
  baked, 47
  with foie gras and smoked salmon terrine, 176
  in Haida Gwaii halibut and asparagus, 140
  in niçoise-style salad, 84
  poached, for smoked salmon rostis, 45
  yolks, cured, 273

elderflower- and grape-glazed trout, 113

elderflower and strawberry sorbet, 236

elderflower vinegar, 258

elk
  crackers, 163
  with forest flavours, 160–63

escabeche, sidestripe shrimp, 148

espresso martini, 249

F

Feather George (cocktail), 244

fennel
  in clam and corn chowder, 64
  in crab cakes, 111
  in crab cappuccino, 66
  mayonnaise, 274

Appetite by Random House® and colophon are registered trademarks of Penguin Random House LLC.

LIBRARY AND ARCHIVES OF CANADA CATALOGUING IN PUBLICATION
IS AVAILABLE UPON REQUEST.

ISBN: 978-0-14-753027-1
eBook ISBN: 978-0-14-753026-4

Cover and book photography: Makito Inomata
Additional photography: page i: Jenn Dykstra; pages ii, xii, 54, 57: Jeremy Koreski; page iv: Sander Jain; pages xiv, 194, 197, 218: Christopher Pouget; pages 3, 4, 6, 22, 27, 38, 62, 97, 98, 129, 137, 147, 150, 156, 234, 243, 257, 278, 288: Michael Becker; page 12: Christopher Pouget and Duncan Booth; page 14: Peter Jackson; page 79: Derek Cruikshanks; pages 102, 167, 245, 246, 253, 276: Kyler Vos; page 193: Colin Way

PRINTED AND BOUND IN CHINA

Published in Canada by Appetite by Random House®,
a division of Penguin Random House Canada Limited.
www.penguinrandomhouse.ca

10 9 8 7 6 5 4 3 2 1

appetite   Penguin
by RANDOM HOUSE   Random House
Canada